EMOTIONAL INTELLIGENCE FOR BEGINNERS

2 Books in 1: How to Analyze People, Manipulation, Persuasion, Increase Self-Discipline and Cognitive Behavioral Therapy

Nicole Gladwell

© Copyright 2020 by Nicole Gladwell. All right reserved.

The work contained herein has been produced with the intent to provide relevant knowledge and information on the topic on the topic described in the title for entertainment purposes only. While the author has gone to every extent to furnish up to date and true information, no claims can be made as to its accuracy or validity as the author has made no claims to be an expert on this topic. Notwithstanding, the reader is asked to do their research and consult any subject matter experts they deem necessary to ensure the quality and accuracy of the material presented herein.

This statement is legally binding as deemed by the Committee of Publishers Association and the American Bar Association for the territory of the United States. Other jurisdictions may apply their legal statutes. Any reproduction, transmission, or copying of this material contained in this work without the express written consent of the copyright holder shall be deemed as a copyright violation as per the current legislation in force on the date of publishing and the subsequent time thereafter. All additional works derived from this material may be claimed by the holder of this copyright.

The data, depictions, events, descriptions, and all other information forthwith are considered to be true, fair, and accurate unless the work is expressly described as a work of fiction. Regardless of the nature of this work, the Publisher is exempt from any responsibility of actions taken by the reader in conjunction with this work. The Publisher acknowledges that the reader acts of their own accord and releases the author and Publisher of any responsibility for the observance of tips, advice, counsel, strategies, and techniques that may be offered in this volume.

TABLE OF CONTENTS

EMOTIONAL INTELLIGENCE FOR BEGINNERS
How to Analyze People, Gain Self-Discipline and Self-Confidence, Master Your Emotions and Overcome Negativity

Chapter 1 *What Is Emotional Intelligence?* 3
Chapter 2 *The Characteristics Of Emotional Intelligence* 5
Chapter 3 *The Advantages Of Developing Strong Eq Skills In The Workplace* 15
Chapter 4 *Effective Tools And Techniques For Emotional Intelligence For Self-Improvement* 31
Chapter 5 *How To Apply Emotional Intelligence Skills In Everyday Situations* 36
Chapter 6 *Myths Vs. Facts About Eq* 56
Chapter 7 *Frequently Asked Questions* 62
Conclusion 71
Description 72

COGNITIVE BEHAVIORAL THERAPY
Retrain Your Brain, Improve Self-Esteem and Self-Discipline, Learn Emotional Intelligence and Change Your Life

Introduction 76
Chapter 1 *What Is Cognitive Behavioral Therapy?* 77
Chapter 2 *When Is Cognitive Behavioral Therapy Used?* 84
Chapter 3 *What Can Cognitive Behavioral Therapy Treat?* 95
Chapter 4 *Cbt And Unhelpful Thinking Styles* 122
Chapter 5 *Examples Of Cbt* 127
Chapter 6 *Preventing Relapses With Cbt* 141
Conclusion 148
Description 150

EMOTIONAL INTELLIGENCE FOR BEGINNERS

How to Analyze People, Gain Self-Discipline and Self-Confidence, Master Your Emotions and Overcome Negativity

Nicole Gladwell

© Copyright 2020 by Nicole Gladwell. All right reserved.

The work contained herein has been produced with the intent to provide relevant knowledge and information on the topic on the topic described in the title for entertainment purposes only. While the author has gone to every extent to furnish up to date and true information, no claims can be made as to its accuracy or validity as the author has made no claims to be an expert on this topic. Notwithstanding, the reader is asked to do their research and consult any subject matter experts they deem necessary to ensure the quality and accuracy of the material presented herein.

This statement is legally binding as deemed by the Committee of Publishers Association and the American Bar Association for the territory of the United States. Other jurisdictions may apply their legal statutes. Any reproduction, transmission, or copying of this material contained in this work without the express written consent of the copyright holder shall be deemed as a copyright violation as per the current legislation in force on the date of publishing and the subsequent time thereafter. All additional works derived from this material may be claimed by the holder of this copyright.

The data, depictions, events, descriptions, and all other information forthwith are considered to be true, fair, and accurate unless the work is expressly described as a work of fiction. Regardless of the nature of this work, the Publisher is exempt from any responsibility of actions taken by the reader in conjunction with this work. The Publisher acknowledges that the reader acts of their own accord and releases the author and Publisher of any responsibility for the observance of tips, advice, counsel, strategies, and techniques that may be offered in this volume.

CHAPTER 1
What Is Emotional Intelligence?

The Basics of Emotional Intelligence (EQ)

Emotional intelligence is defined as having the skills to understand, empathize, and relate to other people and their emotions in a positive way that improves communication and relationships at work, home, and in the community. It's a powerful way to build healthy connections with people and foster strong relationships. Many employers and community leaders value EQ (emotional quotient or emotional intelligence) as criteria to determine which individuals would make ideal employees and colleagues. Aside from industry and work-related experience, education, and skills related to the job, many employers test potential candidates for their ability to empathize, listen, and understand other people. This is especially important in positions focused on customer service and working closely with clients.

As more awareness of the benefits of EQ emerged, more groups and organizations applied this research in the form of tests to administer to applicants for jobs and positions of various kinds, from customer service in finance and retail to assessing the ability of people to handle difficult situations under pressure when dealing with others in public service positions. Emotional intelligence quickly became considered as a solid way to psychologically measure how well people would perform in certain situations by asking scenario-based questions about how to handle a specific scenario or individual. The answers, once assessed, would indicate how empathetic and self-aware the situation was handled, thus evaluating the individual's level of emotional intelligence.

The History and Research Behind Emotional Intelligence

A concept developed in 1990 by John D. Mayer and Peter Salovey, the term emotional intelligence was given to a set of skills involving social intelligence that embodied a variety of criteria, including the ability to empathize with other people, understand and perceive their emotions and feelings, along with the ability to take appropriate actions in conjunction with their needs. EQ or emotional intelligence also refers to an individual's ability to be self-aware of their feelings and emotions and how these relate to their action, behavior, and how they interact with others. Individuals scoring high in EQ skills were generally found to be better at showing empathy to others without discrimination or indifference while monitoring their behavior and improving the social environment within their control for a better outcome. For this reason and other criteria associated with strong emotional intelligence, people who demonstrate these skills are highly regarded and sought by corporations and community organizations as having the optimal fit for handling the public, clients, colleagues, and dealing with other people in general.

CHAPTER 2
The Characteristics Of Emotional Intelligence

What Are the Main Characteristics of EQ or Emotional Intelligence?

How is emotional intelligence measured, and what criteria must be met to indicate a high or proficient level in EQ? When do a person's personal and career goals align with showing a strong sense of emotional intelligence that would appeal to employers? There four main characteristics that indicate the presence of EQ, as follows:

Self-awareness

Are you able to recognize your own emotions and regulate them well? How well do you understand the impact of your feelings, emotions, and how they affect your behavior and actions? The ability to understand the connection between self-confidence, perceived (and real) weaknesses and strengths, and our emotional expressions related to them can give us a better idea of how we can regulate our behavior and notice the same or similar actions in others. Becoming self-aware gives you the ability to self-assess so that you can better manage and control your activities for the overall benefit of the situation. Self-awareness helps you deal with stressful situations and is ideal for leadership positions. This skill gives you the ability to meet tight deadlines and demands that are challenging. Emotionally charged situations are more comfortable to resolve and respond to in a way that settles hostile and aggressive environments because you can take a moment to assess the situation before speaking.

Self-management

Once you become self-aware, you'll have a better understanding of what issues or situations trigger an emotional response and how to control them better. For example, an impulsive reaction to another person's anger can start a heated discussion or argument, whereas responding in a calm and empathetic manner can reduce and avoid the likelihood of an explosive situation. The term self-management refers to the ability to adapt to changing scenarios, as well as how you react or behave in response to them. People with this skill develop confidence in saying no and standing their ground. They can adapt to changing situations and set boundaries so they can ensure their success. Often, it means being proactive and taking measures to mitigate the possibility of conflict, rather than reacting to it when a situation occurs. If you are self-disciplined and follow through on your promises, and consistently stay on track towards achieving your goals, these attributes are also a sign of self-management.

Empathy
Empathy is at the heart of healthy emotional intelligence, along with the ability to listen and look for emotional cues from other people. We may not always understand why people behave in a certain way. However, we are comfortable viewing the world from a different perspective and recognizing why some people have various opinions and thoughts. Recognizing how a situation or topic can influence the way people react and behave can give us a better idea of how to handle or address individuals or groups of people to improve the outcome. Empathy is essential for understanding different cultures, organizations, and businesses, as the world becomes globalized and more connected through technology. In industry, management and leaders with empathy can secure strong relationships and trust in other people. As a result, more employees are content in the workplace, improving morale and loyalty.

People Skills
Developing good social skills is the backbone of emotional intelligence and the top reason why this attribute is vital to improve and work on continuously. Everyone benefits from effective communication, as it can lead to a greater understanding and allows people to work better together and to pursue their goals. It's more than friendliness: fluid social interaction leads to building long-term relationships, both at work and personal. Communication is an essential part of strengthening emotional intelligence, as it can give you the ability to collaborate with others and work well as a team. Many leaders accomplish their goals because they know how to engage with others to develop strategies for this purpose socially. When they share their passions and speak to others, they have a charismatic approach that draws others together. Developing strong social skills means finding what you have in common and connecting with other people in an organization and to achieve mutual goals.

Motivating Yourself and Others
People with emotional intelligence often have the motivation to accomplish what they set out to do. They are self-starters, which works well with both self-management and awareness. In addition to taking pride in their accomplishments, motivated people aim to inspire others to strive for what they want. If one method doesn't work or fulfill your dream, try another. Persistence is another trait that pairs well with motivation, along with learning, growing, and not being afraid to step outside of the usual to attempt something different and unique. They aren't afraid to embrace a new concept or idea, even if other people disagree initially. This skill helps you shine, and while it improves your life significantly, it also brings people together who need or want something new to aim for or work towards in the long term. Individuals

with vital emotional intelligence often demonstrate motivation and persistence while sharing and inspiring others to do the same.

Relationship Management

How well do you work with other people and manage these relationships? Do you continuously argue or debate others in a group, or try to see aspects of a project or discussion from another person's point of view? Emotional intelligence involves curating mutually beneficial and positive relationships with other people in your professional and personal life. Relationships begin with good communication and making a good impression initially while working to inspire and support others and manage conflict to maintain an overall positive experience. Consider some of the people you know for years, whether you work with them, live nearby in a community, and collaborate on various events or projects. The way you convey your feelings and listen to them makes a significant impact on how well your relationship will develop and last over a long period. Inconsistent listening, interrupting, and uncontrollable emotional responses can deter and lessen the positive nature of these connections. Managing relationships includes always being mindful of the other person and responding appropriately by reading emotional cues and other non-verbal (and verbal) signs of communication.

How to Establish Emotion Regulation and Awareness (in Children and Adults)

From a young age, we may recall instances where our emotions overrode our ability to respond logically. Toddlers and young children often express their feelings in outbursts or sudden reactions without any moderation on how they react, simply because they are too young to do so. As we grow into adulthood, improper regulation and processing of our emotions can lead to a lack of social awareness and an inability to every day our behavior and actions. While everyone struggles with serious situations that evoke strong feelings now and again, severe cases where there is no regulation can lead to specific individuals with the inability to function normally in society or hold a regular job.

- Be aware of your (and your child's) emotions. Recognize a feeling and why it is present. Is there a specific reason for feeling a certain way, due to experience or sense? If there is a cause or trigger, acknowledge this and determine the next step, which may be to avoid or address it. When emotion cannot be avoided, allow your child to discuss it with you, then determine the best way to express it. The way we act or behave is an extension of our emotions, and while we can't control what we feel, we can monitor and decide how we express them.
- Acknowledge the emotion and view it as an opportunity to understand your child and yourself better. How often do we try

to quash a feeling because it is uncomfortable or intense? Sometimes emotions are challenging to get through and can arise at inconvenient times. When this happens, it's essential to work through them and recognize why they occur, so that the underlying cause or trigger can become the focus of action.
- Give your emotion a name or validate in some way that makes it real for you. When the same feeling returns, it will resonate with its name or identify, and make it easier to connect with a specific situation or circumstance. This gives you greater control over what causes the emotion to occur initially. If it is a pleasant feeling, you may want to encourage more of the same scenario that is associated with it. In contrast, if it is unpleasant, you may want to avoid or take steps to resolve a negative situation that triggers it.
- Talk about your emotion. Children should be encouraged to do the same. The more we speak out about our feelings, the more equipped we'll be at handling complicated feelings and working through them, instead of pretending they don't exist or suppressing them. Studies have shown that children who don't receive recognition for their emotions or who have been told to hide feelings of sorrow and anger, for example, often grow into adulthood without the proper tools to regulate and control these emotions. This can lead to severe problems with impulsive behavior and a lack of anger management.
- Learn to accept all emotions while understanding that the resulting behaviors are not always acceptable or appropriate. For example, if you feel extreme anger about a person or situation, in a case where injustice has occurred, it is sufficient to feel rage and anger. However, it would be inappropriate to express it with violence or abusive language.

Most people have a better handle on their behavior, which stems from emotions, once they recognize the reasons for their reactions and gain better control over them. When we experience a feeling, it can be the result of a recent incident or situation or originate from a much deeper-rooted experience or recurring problem that has developed over time. Much like the evolution of specific conditions and experiences we encounter as we grow, our emotions also create and can alter the way we communicate with other people and in society in general.

The Development of Emotional Intelligence in Childhood

EQ skills and development begin at an early age, and as we reflect on our childhood or notice traits in our kids. As we learn about the world around us, our internal mechanisms for detecting emotions, understanding the way (and reasons) people act a certain way, and how to interact with them develop at a young age. The sooner a child develops emotional intelligence, the better they will be at developing coping strategies and handling difficult, confrontational situations at school and in early adulthood. While most children will exhibit signs of EQ in the early years, it's essential to realize that everyone develops at their own pace, and in various ways. In some children, emotional advancement may take longer, while others are quick to show a higher EQ than the average child. Even in adulthood, not everyone has the same skill level, nor will each person demonstrate comparable emotional intelligence.

What are some of the early signs of EQ skills? You may notice early signs of emotional intelligence in a child, or may recall some of the following traits from your childhood:

- A child with a strong EQ is more apt to talk about their emotions. They're not afraid to express when they're sad, angry, or scared, and when they do, it's done with a mix of words and non-verbal gestures. By communicating with children and encouraging them to talk more freely, they won't feel the need to hide their feelings, but instead, express them in a healthy, balanced manner.
- In addition to talking about how they feel, a child with a strong understanding of their feelings will be able to identify specific emotions and connect them to certain events or thoughts. For example, they will know that visiting a friend or grandparents is an event that makes them happy while arguing with a friend at school can make them feel frustrated or sad. Attaching thoughts and connections between an incident and an emotion gives a child a better sense of what makes them feel a certain way. If they know that a particular situation makes them feel nervous or unhappy, they may express the effect it has on them and decide how they will handle or communicate as a result. Not all children will talk about the connection they have between individual people, events, things, and their emotions. However, they can develop and understand more as they develop and grow.
- The recognition of emotion on facial expressions or non-verbal gestures is another way in which children can identify and react to other people's emotions. They may develop this ability as they learn to understand their feelings; they will notice the same in others and understand them right away. A young child can point at a person's facial expression in a photo or person and have an idea of what they might be feeling or thinking. The earlier a child notices and understands facial gestures and body language, the easier it will be for them to read cues as they grow into adulthood and develop strong communication skills.

- Identifying an emotion, feeling, and understanding its source is an integral part of comprehending the connection between what you think and why. This is a stepping-stone for developing the ability to avoid potentially harmful situations that have a negative emotional impact while learning how to articulate and react to them. Children who identify these emotions in themselves develop tools for improving their social skills and how to respond to others who exhibit certain emotions or indicate them through non-verbal cues.
- Once children understand others' emotions, they can develop ways to empathize with them and see from another perspective. This is done by applying what they already know about their feelings and how to translate these in communicating their understanding of others. Children with empathy often show kindness and care for others. They will bring home an injured animal and develop a strong bond with pets and other children. If they see someone sad or suffering, they want to understand the source of their pain and cheer them up.
- A child with strong EQ skills may not seem to react emotionally at all or have a delayed response. This is because they are processing what they feel and are taking the time to figure out how they will behave or act as a result.

Children develop emotional intelligence at various stages in their younger years, and while some exhibit signs in caring and understanding each other's emotions sooner than others, their upbringing and exposure to family members with EQ can have an impact on how well they develop. It begins with a simple observation of another child's facial expression or reaction to an incident. Social skills are another vital part of a child's development, and while some kids are slower to cultivate friendships with others, even someone hesitant to make connections can feel for others and detect emotional reactions from a young age.

Developing Emotional Intelligence and How to Apply it at Work, Home, and in Your Community

Emotional intelligence is natural for some individuals to display traits of empathy and good listening skills from a young age. For other people, these skills can be developed and improved over time, with the ability to recognize how they can be enhanced and putting these skills into action. Working towards enhancing EQ skills not only makes a good impression on your next prospective employer, but it can also strengthen the personal relationships you have with family, friends, and neighbors. There are required methods in which emotional intelligence can be developed:

Good Listening Skills
When we listen to someone, how well do we absorb what they say, and do we also note and acknowledge their emotional state of mind and behavior as well? For many people, the act of listening isn't fully understood, and it is common for people to hear the other person without truly understanding them. How many people simply wait until it is their time to speak without fully hearing what the other person is saying? Good listening skills entails more than your presence during a conversation; it involves actively engaging by using body language, gestures, and other motions that indicate that you are actively taking in what the other person is saying. If you don't understand something, instead of dismissing the comment, ask for clarification. Not only does this give the other person a good impression of your listening ability, but it also shows active interest by wanting to know more.

Mindfulness
The act of mindfulness embodies both social and emotional awareness. This entails knowing and understanding how what you say and react will impact the people within your immediate circle at work, home, or community. Mindfulness is also essential for assessing social situations outside of our regular groups and thinking before we speak. This includes considering other people's culture and beliefs before responding and demonstrating what you know about them, what you've learned, and intend to learn. Keeping an open mind means expanding our capacity to learn and adapt to changing situations and understanding that one way of communication may work in one group or social circle, but not in another. Observing the flow of reaction and emotion in an individual or without a group of people can give you a good sense of how well received you are. Mindfulness plays hand in hand with good listening skills because it places the onus on us to make sure we understand what the other person is saying while being observant of how they interact with us when we respond.

Developing Empathy
Understanding how the other person feels and what they are going through is vital to building strong EQ skills. When you empathize, you relate to someone on a personal level. This may seem uncomfortable at first if you're not keen on getting close to someone, though it can have the benefit of easing the other person's concerns and giving them a sense of comfort. "I know it must be hard what you're going through," and "I can understand how frustrating you must feel right now" are good examples of how you can establish an empathetic tone with someone. You can further expand on these examples by relating a personal experience that connects to an individual and their situation, such as losing your wallet or struggling with paying the bills or experiencing a tragic loss.

Being Present and Paying Attention to Others' Needs
Focusing on the present and paying attention to other people and their needs is a primary source of emotional intelligence. When you listen to other people and what they have to say, giving your full attention is more than exercising good listening skills. It involves putting aside any expectations of the future and not focusing on the past, as this can mar the current state of communication. Giving your undivided attention lets the other person know that you are fully present and not distracted by anyone or anything else at that moment. It gives them the potential to completely express themselves and feel comfortable that you will take them seriously. Being present is also about connecting with the other person or group fully, without any reservation.

Common Effects of Emotional Intelligence

EQ skills can be developed to work in many situations, and while it provides a wealth of benefits to your personal and professional development, there are some important aspects of emotional intelligence that should be considered as well. For many people who develop social skills and understand the underlying emotional reasons behind other people's behavior, the situation can be exhausting sometimes. Knowledge and application of emotional intelligence can have a significant impact on the way we process information cognitively, the way we make decisions in life:

- Emotional intelligence impacts every decision in life. You will think before you make a choice about yourself and other people. This is a definite advantage, as it can help you avoid making hasty decisions when it comes to financing, family, and careers.
- You may experience higher levels of stress associated with empathy and getting involved with other people's lives, even if you are able to separate yourself from it. Many people can weigh us down with their emotions, even when there is no intention to cause distress. There can be an increased effect on physical health, and stress management should become a part of your lifestyle. Eating balanced meals and exercise are important ways to maintain good health and handle difficult situations. The direct impact on your well-being can cause side effects such as indigestion, muscle pain, headaches, and fatigue. For this reason, it's important to take care of your physical and emotional health often, as the impact of employing your EQ skills can take a toll over time.
- Connecting with people and understanding their emotional needs can allow you to feel more compassion for others, which can work well in an intimate relationship. In fact, making improvements to your EQ skills can make a major shift in any relationship, and in some cases, it can save family or marriage too. Emotional

intelligence in a relationship can mean several important factors that make your connection stronger:
- You see the full picture and focus on the future. This can provide relief to your partner if they feel insecure about the direction of the relationship or where they stand.
- A rational, calm approach goes a long way to resolve difficult and sensitive issues.
- Using an empathetic response and good listening skills can diffuse an angry situation or where there is volatility. While this can be an emotionally exhausting experience, it can result in peace and better relations in the future.

- Every thought counts as a valid point. When you dwell on something too long, it can feel draining if it weighs on your mind for an extended time. Thoughts have value, and they are where action follows. Thinking too much without taking action can turn a positive thought into a more sinister or negative idea. You may regret not taking a step sooner or overthink. Take each item into consideration and weigh their importance appropriately.
- Emotional intelligence has the potential to be used both ethically and without ethics. Some people use EQ to manipulate others to gain the upper hand and convince them to believe inaccuracies or lies. This can be used by people in business, so-called friends who pretend to be sincere, though have less than altruistic plans. Even where you may use EQ for good, another person can use similar techniques against you as well, which makes it important to focus on any ulterior motives that may play a role in the process. On the other hand, if you are unaware of your emotions, you can become vulnerable to people who manipulate you as well. EQ is a delicate balance between understanding your emotions and guarding against being vulnerable to others.
- Emotional intelligence will leave you with a lot to contemplate. Emotions often influence our thinking and make an impact on how we react, even when we use reasoning and logic. Awareness about how we react emotionally and how we feel makes a significant impact on behavior as well. EQ skills can make you dig deeper and evaluate more in your life. You may wind up with more questions than answers, though in the long term, there is a lot to learn and understand.

Getting acquainted with your EQ ability can take time, though you will experience a great deal of change within. Emotional intelligence will give you a new way to look at the way you communicate with people and handle situations. Most people change when they realize the potential of their ability to understand themselves and others on a clear, more honest level. While there are some challenges to developing EQ and using the skills wisely, it's also a great benefit for making stronger connections at work and home.

CHAPTER 3
The Advantages Of Developing Strong Eq Skills In The Workplace

Employers and Emotional Intelligence: The Pros and Cons of Measuring EQ in Prospective Employees

Over the past few decades, the EQ component in assessing candidates for employment and its importance in the workplace has expanded to include small businesses and organizations to large corporations. Generally, the practice is well received and considered a valuable, if not essential, skill to have to be considered a position within a company. Specific industries that focus primarily on customer and client relations, such as banking and technology, integrate testing and questions about empathy and handling demanding customers into the interview and application process. While many companies and experts in this field alike agree with this practice, there are noted concerns and drawbacks to including EQ as a measurement of skill within the application process.

If you applied for a position, chances are you've taken an EQ test as a part of your assessment. Many employers incorporate this test as a way to assess your emotional intelligence and how it relates to the position applied for. This is often done along with the initial application process when the resume and cover letter are submitted. Employers want to know how a prospective employee will react to a challenging situation or conflict on the job. Amen EQ test will also indicate how well a person can handle criticism, work with other people, and perform other tasks related to their job, including the following:

- Collaborating with individuals and working within a team. How well can they handle and accept different points of view and manage a variance in opinion?
- How well can they adapt to change and accept it as part of an ongoing plan?
- How effective can they communicate with others and contribute to the progression of a project and resolving problems?
- Is a prospective employee likely to become part of the solution and proactively look to avoid pitfalls, or simply complain or cause more problems?

The social skill level of a candidate is a significant factor in determining how to fit a person is for the job, especially where a position requires a considerable amount of interaction with colleagues and clients. Is an employee more likely to inflate a situation with a demanding client, instead of resolving it? Can they find alternative solutions that can improve the relationship between staff, management, and or clients? A person with vital emotional intelligence can proactively listen to a concern and complaint while thinking of a solution and showing empathy. This also involves good listening skills and gives a clear indication that they are actively engaged as well. An individual with high EQ skills can quickly negotiate and work with constructive feedback instead of taking it personally.

Studies indicate that people with good emotional qualities and balance. A person with emotional intelligence will naturally empathize with other people and connect with their feelings more easily. This works well within a team where a solid bond and working relationship can develop. Not only will these individuals succeed in a group, but they will also thrive and contribute significantly, which makes them an asset to a company or organization. They are more apt to accept their weaknesses and use their strengths to enhance their performance while supporting others. Aversions with high EQ skills are also aware of how people with lower social abilities may struggle with emotional intelligence and understand how to interact with them as well. How do employers position questions and scenarios to determine which candidates will be a good fit for the job? The following section provides examples of what to expect during an interview for your next job.

Questions and Scenarios for Interviews

Whether your prospective employer may implement a series of questions to evaluate your emotional intelligence, there are a few ways this can be done. Some companies provide a standard multiple-choice format, with a list of questions and a selection of answers to choose from for each. This questionnaire may be provided at the preliminary application stage or the first interview. In some cases, an employer might wait until the second interview to determine your EQ skills. This may be due to prioritizing other attributes as the first level of qualifications, then using the emotional intelligence quiz or questions as a second stage filter. The strategy by which an employer may decide to assess EQ varies from one organization or company to the next. A job in customer service, for example, may focus more on emotional intelligence than a tech-based position where interaction with others is less frequent.

Questions that assess emotional intelligence, when included as part of the interview process, tend to be scenario-based, such as the following examples:

- If you were tasked with resolving a conflict between two colleagues or coworkers, how would you approach the situation? What steps would you take?

- Have you ever received criticism about your performance or work? How did you respond, and what did you learn from the experience?
- Think about a dilemma you faced on the job that involved ethics. How did you handle the situation?
- Sometimes customers will complain about a product or service. How would you handle this situation?
- Consider a time when you encountered a conflict with a supervisor or manager. How did you initially respond, and how did you resolve the situation? What did you learn from the experience?
- Imagine a scenario where you are promoting a campaign about our products. A customer quickly complains about the service or product to you directly. How do you handle the situation?

These questions are merely a sample of what to expect in an interview. Some employers will look for a range of responses, and in addition to your response, they will take note of body language and non-verbal cues. How long did you take to respond? Can you think of a relevant situation that comes to mind quickly, order it take some time? Interviewers understand the importance of giving the candidate enough time to reflect before replying with a relevant scenario and solution. During this time, they may read your facial expressions and determine how your reaction to their question may play a role in your response. Employers may also provide a hypothetical situation and ask how you would handle the problem. This gives the candidate an opportunity to visualize and consider how they would resolve a potential challenge, even if their experience is limited, as the response would indicate their level of EQ. Consider some of the following scenarios an interviewer may propose for your input and a solution:

1. An employer will describe a scenario that could relate to their personal experience and may resemble a situation that the candidate may encounter on the job, such as facing an angry customer or unethical colleague or coworker. They may give you a few details to work with that may help or hinder the circumstances. This gives the candidate a clear picture of what they have to work with. During this discussion, further questions that pinpoint the extent of EQ skills may include:
    a. And what if (another situation or complication occurs during the incident)
    b. Have you encountered or faced a similar incident with a colleague or client?
    c. What was the lasting result of the final outcome of the event?

       d. Why did the situation happen in the first place? In your opinion, what could have been done to prevent it?
       e. What did you learn from the experience?
       f. Did the colleague or client change after?
2. The interviewer may pay attention to body language during the response. This includes examining your initial gestures or facial expressions upon being asked the question.
3. A scenario-based question that specifically relates to a company-based situation may also be asked, either in place of a hypothetical, general question or in addition to it. This will give the employer a better idea of how you would handle a more probable situation that could likely occur on a typical working day.

How does an employer assess how to gauge the level of emotional intelligence based on the responses given by the candidate? It's important to realize that while emotional intelligence is at the heart of these questions, its importance doesn't apply equally in all scenarios presented. For example, a salesperson may explain how they didn't respond to a complaint because it didn't bother them, or simply gave them credit or discount to appease them or avoid having to deal with the client. While this resolution may seem favorable to both the customer and the company, the process does not include empathizing with the client. Sometimes, a salesperson or representative may delay responding to a complaint from a client. This may be due to finding a situation or several alternatives before offering them. An immediate response can be premature and will not satisfy the needs of the customer. Taking a bit of time, within reason, maybe the best option, and it will let the client know that you made an effort to resolve the problem, instead of trying to convince them otherwise.

Placing yourself in the customer's position is the best way for a candidate to articulate a response that involves empathy. Some clients want to be heard and acknowledged for their complaints or issues, while others prefer a discrete approach. This can vary depending on the situation and how delicate the matter is. Taking all these factors into consideration is one way you can make amends with a broken client relationship, and let them know that they are essential. Looking for signs of empathy and taking the time to find the most suitable solution are ways in which an interviewer will assess the level of emotional intelligence involved.

What are some of the red flags or indicators that there is a lack of EQ skills? Some candidates may display some warning signs more openly than others. Sometimes, a subtle gesture or comment is all that's needed to hint at a lack of social skills. If an employer sees potential in a candidate and a willingness to learn and adapt, they may consider hiring them on a trial basis, especially if they show promise in other skills. This situation also depends on the company and line of work the employee is meant to perform. The following signs may indicate a candidate is not a good fit for employment, especially if they are expected to work with many clients and colleagues:

- If a candidate brushes the issue aside and generalized their response, such as "I spoke with my colleague, and we came to an agreement," or "I know how to get along with other people" and "I take clients and their needs seriously," this can be a lack of social and emotional intelligence. A candidate should be expected to elaborate or give a specific example of what they mean. How do they get along with their colleagues? Give an example of how a client relationship was restored after receiving a complaint, and so on.
- Short, canned responses that seem rehearsed are another reason to consider a lack of EQ skills. If this is the only type of reply a potential employee can provide, what does this say about their personal and professional experience? Do they simply lack the real, hands-on experience needed for the job, or only looking for the most straightforward answer to get the job?
- Self-management and how we manage our relationships with others is another important way to assess the value of EQ in an individual. Do they make a complaint about their previous or current coworkers' colleagues or boss? Do you get the impression the only reason they applied for the job is to avoid dealing with other people with whom they do not work well with? On the other hand, if an employee indicates that a mismanagement relationship was resolved and improved over time, including behavioral modifications, this can demonstrate their ability to handle difficult people and circumstances, which makes them the right candidate for the job.
- Does a candidate shift with discomfort when an interviewer asks about a subject or situation that involves emotional intelligence? Are they generally avoidant and demonstrate poor impulse control in the way they answer questions and conduct themselves during the interview? This is a clear indication that they may not be fit to handle stressful scenarios on the job or perform well under pressure. They may assure you they can meet deadlines and get things done, but they struggle in real-life situations.

Interviewers and human resources professionals are well versed in what to look for in a candidate. Emotional intelligence is highly regarded as an essential skill to have in a variety of positions. While some people consider the drawbacks in assessing EQ skills, most employers, including human resources professionals and companies, regard them as an essential tool for measuring the level of fitness for the job and ability to collaborate within a team.

The Advantages

Considering the many advantages to hiring employees with vital emotional intelligence, and the potential to employ a more empathetic and well-developed team, many employers consider the following benefits:

- Employees with self-awareness and good management skills tend to be excellent at working independently and with little or no supervision. They are usually good with self-management and often display strong self-discipline, which is not only a positive trait for productivity and business but also an excellent example for other employees to follow.
- Good listening skills translate into networking well with colleagues, stakeholders, and customers. People are more apt to take you seriously and listen to you if you pay attention to their needs as well. Exercising strong listening skills can make the difference between losing and closing a sale, for example, or de-escalating a severe disagreement or situation.
- People with high emotional intelligence are less prone to angry outbursts and are typically easier to talk within general. They are good problem solvers and usually think and act proactively, often negotiating and working with other people to set a positive standard and avoid conflict before it happens.
- There is evidence of improved physical and psychological health among people with more robust emotional intelligence. This is because they know when to recognize a destructive habit and how it ties into their emotional state. For example, if you are a chronic smoker or overeat due to stress, you'll realize the danger of stressful situations and take action to reduce and manage this aspect of your life, therefore decreasing the chances of adverse reactions and self-destructive habits. You'll make healthier choices in general and take note of any erratic options or mood changes when they occur. A healthier lifestyle leads to less risk of heart disease, cancer, and other debilitating conditions.
- You can be emotionally healthy and reliable while demonstrating a keen sense of sensitivity and care for others. Often, it is assumed that demonstrating emotional intelligence means you cannot be mentally "tough." This is not the case, as showing empathy and sensitivity towards others while keeping your own emotions in check indicates a strong sense of awareness and a high degree of control. This is an ideal attribute in the workplace, especially when dealing with a contentious situation, where a calm, negotiation-like approach is needed.

Developing a good set of skills is never easy, and while some people are naturally better at having strong EQ abilities, it's a worthwhile endeavor for everyone to strive for in life. There are no shortcuts or quick ways around it. Some people debate the legitimacy of emotional intelligence, though it's a real, tangible method of making the most for you and other people in life.

The Disadvantages

There are some disadvantages to relying on emotional intelligence, though this relates mostly to focusing on these skills beyond the scope of their importance. While EQ is a vital set of skills for success in business and career growth, too much focus on it and not enough consideration of other traits can spell other problems or issues that may be encountered as follows:

- The right employee or staff for the job may not be healthy in emotional intelligence, though they can meet (or exceed) all the qualifications for the job. If the position does not require a high degree of human interaction, measuring EQ skills may not be worth the effort, as other credentials will take priority, such as technical or medical skills and expertise.
- Some employers place too much emphasis on EQ skills and can miss other attributes that are equally or more important. An employee hired to fulfill the requirements of a job may display excellent customer service and good listening skills, though fall short in achieving their role within the position because they lack other vital credentials that are needed.
- Empathy can be inflated by people who want to appear to be high in emotional intelligence falsely. While this is not common, it can be done in circumstances where a candidate for a job is accustomed to this test and wants to impress their prospective employer with strong communication skills. A person who is not usually a good listener and lacking in EQ skills could pretend or convince someone otherwise if they genuinely wanted to gain favor and a chance at getting the job. They may display charm or use flattery to impress someone, which may appear that they are interested in you and understand your feelings, though it's merely a tactic to gain favor and get what they want.
- Emotional intelligence is often misunderstood as being emotionally sensitive, which is wrongly defined as "weak." Making a strong connection with someone's feelings takes a lot of understanding and awareness. You can relate to another person on an emotional level without losing control of your feelings. The idea that expressing one's feelings is a sign of weakness has caused many people to suppress their emotions, which causes more difficulties in how they manage their behaviors and actions that

stem from them. In recent years, the idea of developing EQ skills has become better understood as a sign of strength, not weakness, and this will continue as the benefits improve many relationships at work and in personal situations.
- Some people who rank high in emotional intelligence may know the assessment criteria well and have no difficulty in passing the test, as they know how to respond. While this is not a reason to view EQ skill testing as less adequate or reliable, it is not uncommon for some candidates to appear socialized in one aspect and to lack in another. For example, a person can make an excellent first impression and show a high degree of engagement and attention to others' emotions, though this can quickly change over time with various situations.
- The way a person reacts in a difficult situation or with a challenging client or colleague truly indicates their ability to use EQ skills and empathy. A test can give an employer a glimpse or idea of an individual's ability to handle a scenario, though the true nature of a person is revealed just once they must face a dilemma in real life.

Considering both the advantages and disadvantages of assessing the attributes of emotional intelligence in candidates, years of reason and practical application have sided in favor of its use. Employers have implemented EQ-related questions into first and second interviews, questionnaires with scenario-based questions, and other exercises to measure the behavioral reaction and activity an employee would engage in. While these methods do not guarantee that an individual will make the best decisions for every situation, the process eliminates the higher risk of hiring people who would not respond appropriately, and this could increase the liability of a company or organization.

Why Developing EQ Can Help You Find (and Obtain) Your Next Job

Emotional intelligence is key to making a good impression on a prospective employer and demonstrating that you are not only capable of interacting and working well with other people, but also proactive and a good listener. Not only will establishing and developing EQ skills help you land the job, but it will also give you the tools to maintain your position and move in the direction you want. While many other qualifications will determine how well you will advance in your career, emotional intelligence is a vital part of networking and developing long-lasting relationships in business and forming strong connections with clients as well. How can developing EQ skills impress your next employer and help you get hired?

1. An employee should be reliable, and your next employer will want to know that they can count on you to get the job done. Not only does EQ indicate that you have good people skills, but it also unveils that you are self-disciplined and will get the tasks done promptly. Self-regulation and management of your schedule and responsibilities are a significant part of emotional intelligence and indicate a good fit for a supervisory role or position in government.
2. If you are having a bad day at the office or dealing with a disgruntled coworker or client, chances are you will handle it well. When you display a professional and careful approach to resolving issues and addressing them carefully, this maximizes the right optics between you and your employer, which is the ideal scenario. Monitoring and recognizing your emotions and keeping your behavior (and reactions) in check indicate the strength of character that most employers admire and need on the job.
3. You are good at listening to other people without judgment or making them feel disregarded. This is a valuable way to give other people at work and customers a sense of value and care. They are also more likely to listen to you and show the same level of respect in return. Mutual respect leads to working productively together and taking everyone's ideas and input seriously.
4. You'll work better in a team and communicate more effectively. As a result, more people are likely to listen to you and take what you say seriously. Good communication skills are a two-way street, which means you must also demonstrate good listening, which leads to meaningful conversation and better understanding overall.
5. Greater EQ skills mean you'll invest more in a company or team at work because you're willing to connect with more people and develop those relations. This means investing in both time and effort, which leads to tremendous success and results at work.

What does a situation which involves a display of EQ skills entail? What are some examples that illustrate how well an individual can adapt successfully or fail at applying emotional intelligence? The following scenarios provide a glimpse into how each interaction is unique, and there is no single solution for everyone. An adequate explanation for one case may be inefficient for another. Some employers may incorporate questions about emotional intelligence into the interview process while others use a standard questionnaire or test to evaluate the EQ skill level.

Example 1: Conflict between Coworkers
One common phrase many people believe is that the customer is always right. While this may be a standard way of thinking in practice, some salespersons will disagree with this statement, or at least note some

exceptions to the rule. Danielle began work as a sales associate for a printing company. Most customers were small businesses and appeared very loyal to the printing shop. As a result, the store did well, and Danielle was offered more hours than expected, due to an increase in sales. She appeared to have a good rapport with clients. She had ambitions of promoting the shop to new freelancers and area businesses scheduled to open shortly. One such place was a dog grooming shop looking to promote their services throughout the city, bringing as many new clients as possible.

Danielle aimed to secure a contract for hundreds of promotional flyers and business cards. Jon and Fran, the owners of the dog grooming shop, seemed pleased with the proposal, which secured a new client for the shop. Danielle wanted to keep the lead for herself, to maximize commission on their sales. On her day off, Ivy, another sales associate, happened to be in the shop when Jon and Fran visited to finalize their first order. Not knowing the sale originated with Danielle, Ivy recorded the contract under her name and received a commission. When Danielle found out, she was furious, but also realized that she should have noted the potential client as her lead so that this problem could have been avoided. When Danielle discovered that Ivy had taken her sale, she made a scene in the store, even in front of another customer, who quickly left. Ivy calmly explained that had she known Jon and Fran were her sales, she would not have recorded them as her own. Danielle accused Ivy of not asking the dog groomers where they first learned of the printing shop, which was not a requirement. Ivy remained calm and courteous, though I didn't agree with Danielle. She suggested that if Danielle wasn't satisfied with the outcome, that she could take it up with management. In the meantime, Jon and Fran were happy with the printing and requested more flyers and business cards. Danielle would fume every time this occurred, and when she finally faced the couple, she asked them if they remembered speaking with her initially. Ivy was present and noted that they had initially said with Danielle. However, the sales were already made, and there was no reversing the commission from Ivy. Danielle decided to use passive aggression to express her displeasure. She would hide or rearrange product samples and avoid talking to Ivy, giving her the silent treatment. Eventually, the situation became unbearable, and Ivy ended up quitting upon finding a better paying job. Management was disappointed to see Ivy leave, and when they conducted an exit interview to find out why, she hesitated to admit that the main reason was Danielle. She was surprised to find out that other people experienced difficulties with Danielle too, and some had left previously or avoided working with her as much as possible. Ivy was stunned because no one had mentioned it to her. Danielle displayed a lack of empathy towards several customers, which was overlooked because she was new, and the manager felt she deserved another chance. Ivy would have kept her job if the company had disciplined Danielle, but in their failure to do so, they lost Ivy and provided a stern warning to Danielle, who did not take it well.

Over the following couple of months, sales were steady, and Danielle secured new contracts. Two new employees were hired to work part-time. Danielle was given a raise and instructed to train and support them in their roles. Initially, the process went well, though Danielle was determined to assert a supervisory role over the two new staff members, who were afraid to complain to management. This impacted their ability to perform, and once again, Danielle was left as the one employee no one would work with, despite her success with clients and sales.

Outcome and Assessment of Example 1

Danielle was a prize employee of the printing shop, though it did not work well with other staff. This situation created a hostile work environment that resulted in high turnover and great dissatisfaction from other staff. Danielle was excellent with clients but did not work well with her colleagues. Once she passed her probationary period, despite receiving one warning about her mistreatment of Ivy, she rarely spoke to management, and they tried avoiding her as well, as long as sales were stellar and consistent.

Did the management and owners of the printing shop fail their staff? How could they have avoided hiring Danielle, or upon discovering the true nature of her behavior, correct the situation? How could these pitfalls be avoided?

- When Danielle was interviewed and asked to provide examples of how she handled difficult situations in a previous job, she only focused on repairing relationships with customers. An example of how to improve a relationship with a colleague or coworker would have given the interviewer more details. In practice, Danielle was not good at working with other staff and hid this detail well during the interview and application process.
- Working within a team was not Danielle's strength. She only worked well with others when she could have the upper hand and did not take direction well. In a supervisory position, Danielle would thrive, and as long as others would follow her orders and not question her motives. Unfortunately, she clashed with several employees, and as a result, the company lost them to other employment.
- References were a requirement of the application process, which was standard practice at the printing shop. Danielle provided the required three work-related references, though they were all on good terms with her. Some people who do not work well with a person will give a positive referral so that they can "get rid" of

them. This situation was the case with at least two of the three people recorded as references on Danielle's application.

Once an employer hires someone new, they may have performed all the background checks, assessments, and skills for the position. The candidate may appear suitable, even in cases where they are not, which can occur in some instances. In the situation involving Danielle, it became the employer's duty to monitor her performance during the first few months to determine if she would be the right sales associate for the long term. During this period, management neglected to pay close attention and assumed that they hired the right fit, despite complaints from staff, including Ivy, which were ignored. Management made the mistake of assuming every employee, once hired, didn't require further monitoring. This practice became habitual as most staff were satisfactory for their positions and didn't raise any red flags. What they didn't anticipate was the possibility of some issues, which undetected, could lead to higher turnover and a decline in morale.

How can the employer avoid future issues with Danielle and other staff in a similar situation? By checking in with all staff and making sure there is fairness and equal consideration for everyone, the printing store management could have set boundaries and guidelines for employees to follow, and curb any behavior that doesn't create a positive, productive environment for everyone.

Example 2: Assessing the Candidates for the Job

Jake was a human resources associate. He was new in the field of personnel management, though his employer, a medium-sized financial firm, was confident in his ability to assess the first group of applications. The position advertised was for an accounting clerk, which would require some experience and knowledge of the financial field, The firm was willing to accept an individual with the right mindset and ambition to move within the company. A strong ability to work well with other people was mandatory, not because the job entailed working directly with clients or potential clients. However, teamwork and getting along with a variety of coworkers were essential. While the firm initially wanted to hire two employees to work in accounting for the same position, they focused on hiring one to start, then progressing from there. Jake was excited to begin the process of filtering through applications and resumes, knowing this was an important step in his role. He was given a set of criteria to assess each resume and cover letter, which included education, past experience, and other factors, all of the skills related. If an applicant didn't have accounting experience but worked in a retail store as an assistant manager, there was potential, as they would understand budgeting. There were a few other exceptions as well, which Jake was aware of and took seriously. A total of just over one hundred applications were received for the one position, which surprised him. It would be a challenge, though Jake was ready for it.

Many of the applications indicated a background or education in accounting in some capacity, which made reducing the pile of applicants difficult. Jake noticed that while many applicants had a university or college education, not everyone worked in an environment where finances were a part of their job. For example, an assistant property manager may be better suited to an accounting role than someone with more education in the field of financial accounting without practical experience. This perplexed Jake, but he managed to narrow the large group of applications to twenty. The head of human resources asked that the pile be further reduced to ten or less, which would prove difficult. Jake decided that while he could scrutinize the resumes a bit more and reduce them further, this would likely be redundant, as he was well acquainted with their respective qualifications.

Jake thought about his options for reducing the group of applications. Upon serious consideration, he decided to interview them over the phone. This process would not be a formal interview, though it would be a quick session to get to know each of the people. One of the reasons Jake was hired as a human resources associate was due to his excellent social skills and ability to speak to anyone. He could draw a person out to determine their true feelings because they felt comfortable with him. Not all the associates in his department felt a phone interview would work, and that checking for inconsistencies or faults in each of the resumes would be a more practical option. Jake dismissed these ideas and followed his plan instead.

Surprisingly, Jake's plan was a success. Of the first five candidates, he found that only two were suitable and easy to talk to, while the others were hesitant and unprepared. Working further down the list of twenty applicants, Jake soon found eight that would make a great accounting clerk and was ready for the next step, to schedule the first official interview. Of the eight applicants remaining, five were scheduled for interviews with a panel of staff, including management and human resources. The remaining three candidates quickly found other employment, which narrowed down the list to a smaller group. Jake was eager to meet each of the candidates and prepared a questionnaire to gauge their fitness for the job further. He read and studied a lot about emotional intelligence, and based on the culture of the company; he knew this aspect of the job was most important, outside of standard skills and qualifications for the job. All the interviews were scheduled in one day. Jake gave each of the candidates a simple written test to complete prior to their interview, then took notes on his thoughts and feedback, based on both their written results and interview performance:

Candidate 1: David

David worked as a temporary project manager for a firm for a period of six months. He was involved with community engagement, working with a couple of organizations that focused on helping people in need. This gave him a good work-life balance and highlighted his ability to work with a wide variety of people. He didn't have an accounting background, though he worked with budgets and displayed a good understanding of math and recordkeeping.

Candidate 2: Stacy
Stacy had a background working as a nurse's aide in health care and displayed a strong passion for people. She took a couple of courses in financial accounting before deciding to switch into the medical field. Her ability to relate well to other people was impressive. While she knew to account too, she was quick to interrupt a couple of times. She appeared to be nervous during the interview, though overall, her social skills and qualifications were well received by everyone.

Candidate 3: Rodney
Rodney was professional and straight-forward from the start. He was quick to explain his goals for studying to become a certified financial advisor and hoped this position would give him the platform to build his career. He was good at striking up a conversation with one or two of the panelists before the official interview began. Everyone seemed content with his goal-oriented personality, and while he was charismatic and easy to get along with during the interview, the questionnaire he completed about scenario-based EQ skills seemed a bit vague and difficult to ascertain whether he would be a good fit in the company's social culture.

Candidate 4: Amy
A recent graduate from university, Amy was eager to start an entry-level job in accounting, considering she majored in economics. It was a good opportunity for her career. She did not have prior work experience and was much younger than the other candidates. Amy worked briefly in a retail store over one summer, though the hours were casual, and she couldn't provide any references to support her application. She seemed eager to please and answered the questionnaire with good responses, indicating how she would take a problem-solving approach to each scenario and try to look at other people's perspectives during the process.

Candidate 5: Stan
Stan was experienced in a few areas of work and was the oldest candidate with his job history, including both retail and wholesale sales, while managing a small business on the side. He was ready to take on a full-time job and enjoyed working with numbers. While he didn't have any education in accounting, specifically, Stan was willing to take courses to improve his skills and make a difference in his job. He was easy-going, and while the questionnaire was answered well, he appeared reserved

and quiet mostly, which made it difficult to determine how he would fit in socially.

On various levels, all the candidates showed potential, and Jake found the process of picking just two for the final, second interview daunting. Before scheduling the second interview, he needed to eliminate three of the candidates from the list. Instead of dwelling on the applicants who would be removed from the list, Jake focused on the two that would make the best fit for the position. He needed to consult with the rest of the team (both human resources and management) to determine which two people would be the finalists. The following ideas were considered during a few discussions between the group:

- The candidate should be strong in math and feel confident about performing various accounting procedures on the computer, though the tasks are simple and shouldn't be too difficult for most candidates to handle. For this reason, someone with accounting experience would be ideal.
- New software systems will be introduced to the company, and this will require working together closely with teammates to train and support each other. Employees with strong emotional intelligence are especially needed for this purpose.
- In the long term, due to new upgrades in the company's system, less manual accounting entries and reports would be needed, and attention to detail and collaborating with other teams and colleagues would become a priority.

In reviewing all the qualifications for the job, and the ever-changing workplace, Jake finalized his decision to include Amy and Stan, as they both embodied traits that the firm was looking for. Stan was older, had a wealth of knowledge and experience, while Amy was newer to the workforce, though they demonstrated a sincere eagerness to learn and progress. Jake had another reason for choosing the two candidates for hire: he noticed both of them met in the elevator on the way to the interview and introduced each other. Despite their different backgrounds, they discovered a few common goals that they shared. The firm was settled on adding just one employee, though due to a sudden increase in work volume, both candidates were offered a position in the interim, to determine their performance and fitness for the job.

Outcome and Assessment of Example 2

Jake was confident in his decision to hire the two candidates, Amy and Stan, for the accounting department. Their employment with the company began with an introduction to the team and getting familiar with the accounting system and computer process. They both asked a lot of questions and were eager to begin training. Jake's human resources team was pleased with the results, though concerned about how well two new hires would fit into a progressive, forward-thinking group of people who shared extensive experience in both accounting and working at the firm. Jake explained how both Amy and Stan, while vastly different from each other and the rest of the accounting team, showed a positive attitude and seemed to fit into the company right away. He further mentioned how human resources and management would need to check in with accounting periodically to monitor the new employees and the rest of the team. Productivity was important, though morale and the loyalty of staff were also vital.

Applying Emotional Intelligence in the Workplace

Assessing EQ skills at the recruitment and selection phase is important; however, making sure the new employees demonstrate these skills throughout their career with a company or organization is equally, if not more important, in the long term. As more people become familiar with EQ testing, it can become easier to answer questions with the answers that an employer wants to hear or see, rather than accuracy. Some employers disregard the EQ skills testing with this in mind: they realize candidates can manipulate the process to some degree, and gain favor with an interviewer to increase their chances of getting the job. Once hired, they may demonstrate characteristics that differ from their initial impression. Over time, this trend, while not too common, prompted more employers to change the nature of assessing candidates to include more detailed responses. Instead of asking them how they would respond to a specific scenario, they ask them to provide an example from their personal or professional experience where emotional intelligence skills were applied. This approach places the onus on the candidate to not only to consider which example to provide, but how they proactively resolved an issue.

CHAPTER 4
Effective Tools And Techniques For Emotional Intelligence For Self-Improvement

Making a Better Impression and Improving Your EQ Level

The level of emotional intelligence varies in everybody, from individuals who are naturally healthy in EQ skills and those who are entirely unaware of how their behavior and actions, fueled by emotion, affect other people. For many people, there are some skills present, while others can be developed and improved over time. Recognizing the need to improve and understand the importance of EQ is the ideal starting point and where to begin. People with all levels of emotional intelligence can benefit from making improvements to their skills:

1. Think before you speak. Are you feeling stressed or facing an uncertain situation that may evoke a strong emotional response? This scenario happens to everyone, and while some cases are challenging to manage, taking a moment to breathe deeply and decide what to say can save you from making a significant blunder. Reacting too quickly can cause more distress and escalation than necessary. It can also lead to misunderstanding, which can lead to a breakdown in communication.
2. Build self-management skills. Are you good at managing how you pace yourself when addressing situations on the job and at home? Can you decide with careful assessment of how your emotions may or may not play a role? Even people with EQ skills need to work on self-management as our circumstances in life continuously change. Being aware of your emotional state during a difficult situation or receiving bad news will help you react appropriately and cope as well. Keeping our emotions and feelings in check can be a challenge, though it will give you time to process a situation that requires reflection. Managing how we react and communicate with other people will build strong, reliable relationships.
3. Becoming self-aware and reflecting on our actions is an integral part of observing your actions and how they impact other people. Many emotions we experience are rooted in childhood, including strong feelings towards certain situations or events that can trigger a reaction quickly. Similarly, when we communicate with other people, it's important to recognize when a comment or phrase affects you or someone else. Are you aware of a reaction or gesture that indicates discomfort in someone else? Do you experience anxiousness or a sudden shift in feelings when

someone makes a specific comment? Understanding the connection between our emotions, how we react or respond, and the world around us is vital to improving coping mechanisms and strategies for dealing with difficult situations. Recognizing how our behavior impacts other people can allow us to avoid certain tactics that can trigger a negative emotion or response in someone else.
4. Practice mindfulness and become aware of how you feel at the moment. When you converse with someone, notice how they react and how they use non-verbal cues to express their true feelings. Paying attention to the way other people communicate and interact with you doesn't mean focusing away from self-awareness. It's possible to be mindful of other people while checking in with your emotions and how you respond. By putting the other person's ideas and feelings first, even momentarily, will increase the benefit of the interaction and further your relationship with them. They will notice your actions as altruistic and empathetic, which builds confidence.
5. Visualize a problem or issue involving one or more people, specifically someone who may be challenging to work or live with and imagine how you would diffuse a situation by using EQ skills. Consider the worst-case scenario: some people will personally attack you and employ insults to make you feel inadequate, and often, to devalue anything you have to say or do to calm the situation. In these situations, it's vital to maintain focus on the main goal and avoid distractions that take away from your power to resolve.

On some level, we all can develop and use emotional intelligence to our benefit, whether we are naturally prone to doing so, or in the process of learning. Emotional intelligence is a skill set that requires ongoing improvement and attention to ensure we can adapt to a wide range of scenarios and circumstances. A long record of empathy and care can be easily derailed with a sudden outburst or lack of restraint, which can occur, especially during an emotionally charged situation. The next chapter focuses on how to identify areas of improvement for EQ skill-building.

How to Recognize Areas for Improvement and Increase Your Emotional Intelligence

Developing emotional intelligence is different for everyone. Some people are naturally prone to empathy, good listening skills, and other traits, there are many skills and ideas that most of us will find useful to improve. Individuals with high EQ can also benefit from continuous awareness and striving to sharpen their social interactions with others. The following techniques are simple ways to engage better in conversation and connection:

- When you encounter conflict, consider it an experience to learn and grow from. Disagreements will happen, and they are common because not everyone shares the same opinions, ideas, or thoughts about everything. Some people will react strongly, even offensively, when you don't align your thinking with theirs. In severe cases where an individual or group makes an offensive statement or ignorant remark, it's natural to react impulsively. It may not be easy to see the constructive side of the worst confrontation. Instead of reaction immediately, and give yourself a few seconds, even a minute. Let the other person contemplate on what they just said and see where it goes. Sometimes, a remark is made in error, and this period of silence allows the other person to correct. Furthermore, avoid seeing conflict as a punishment or a threat, even if it is perceived to be from a specific person. This will give you more freedom to respond thoughtfully, or not at all, under these circumstances. Furthermore, it places the responsibility on the person commenting, as they are left to explain themselves.
- A sense of humor goes a long way to connect with someone. Most people appreciate a light joke or a smile. This can also diffuse a stressful situation, where one or more people dread a conversation or feel as though they are being interrogated. Reducing stress and keeping the atmosphere calm and pleasant can give the other person a sense that you understand them and want to extend a warm welcome. It gives you a chance to break the ice, especially during a tense interaction. If you're nervous, inserting a bit of humor can relieve your stress and make it easier to communicate.
- Be aware of your non-verbal cues and gestures, as they can send the wrong message or confuse the person or group you are speaking to. For example, if you want to appear welcoming and accepting, folding your arms across your chest and averting eye contact indicate the opposite intention. If you want to make a connection with someone, but avoid them regularly, either because you are nervous or uncertain of how they will respond, you'll lose the opportunity completely. If you're not sure how to approach someone, smile, and nod in their direction to give them a friendly introduction. Their reaction will usually indicate if they are interested.

How Non-verbal Communication Can Improve Emotional Intelligence

It is not uncommon to say something we don't mean, though this is not always done will ill intentions. There may be a reason we agree with someone's opinion, even if we see fault in it, or say yes when we experience hesitation inside. How often do you encounter someone who says one thing, though it appears they are not entirely truthful or honest about their feelings? By observing body language and gestures, a person's true thoughts or opinions about a topic or situation are often revealed. For example, someone may verbally express their excitement to attend an event, though their body language indicates they are uncomfortable. They may fold their arms tightly across their chest or avoid looking at anyone, for fear their true feelings may be revealed. On the other hand, a person may act uninterested in a situation so that they don't appear too nosy. However, their body language indicates they are engaged and wouldn't mind learning more about it.

The way we communicate with non-verbal cues and gestures conveys a lot to other people. A person who is considering whether to divulge personal information to a coworker may feel more compelled if they display a warm, relaxed posture and smile often. An individual who seems constantly preoccupied or distracted will not receive the same attention as someone who indicates their interest by making regular eye contact and nodding in the direction of the speaker. Actively showing your interest can make a significant difference in the success of the interaction and how well the other person engages with you. Which type of gestures and body language works best for showing empathy and good listening skills?

- Maintain eye contact regularly, though avoid staring too long, which can appear as though you may not be listening well or make the other person uncomfortable.
- If you are standing during the conversation, avoid folding your arms and, instead, allow your arms to relax by your sides and lean in a bit closer (carefully assessing the comfort zone) and smile.
- Nod often and do so when a comment or point is made. This will give the other person confirmation that you heard and understood what they said.
- Avoid distractions and keep your focus on the person or people in the group. Always face towards the person speaking, and acknowledge each person as the conversation or discussion moves from one person to another
- Even if you are nervous, avoid fidgeting with your hands or looking at your phone. This will give the impression that you are distressed, though it can also make you appear avoidant.

- Don't be afraid to be expressive with body language, because this usually has a positive effect on the people around you. Hand, arm, and facial gestures show you are engaged and involved in the conversation.
- When shaking hands or greeting someone, always make eye contact initially, and use the moment to make a good first impression.
- Pay attention to certain cues about the other person, especially when first meeting with them: do they approach you to shake hands, or do they avoid this exchange? Some people view shaking hands as a common way to greet a new person with professionalism, while others are not comfortable getting too close. If you prefer to skip handshaking, nod, and express that you are happy to meet the other person, as this will often suffice as polite and well-intentioned.

In addition to the above criteria, it's important to become familiar with various cultures and traditions within a certain company, firm, or region. If you travel for business, you'll want to learn which gestures or body language is considered appropriate, and which may be considered offensive. In some cultures, it's acceptable to embrace or move within a close range of personal space, even in some formal business meetings. In contrast, other cultures forbid or discourage close contact of any kind, including handshaking. On a more specific level, certain companies may be known as conservative in how they greet people, while others have a more "chill" or relaxed approach to making a first impression. Conducting research on various companies and cultures is a great way to avoid possible misunderstandings and improve the impression you make on delegates and representatives.

CHAPTER 5
How To Apply Emotional Intelligence Skills In Everyday Situations

Emotional intelligence is often considered a major benefit in the workplace, and for a good reason: it is a vital toolset for selecting the most empathetic team-players for the job. While the importance of EQ skills varies from one job to another, social skills are also important in personal life situations where conflict can arise and escalate quickly. This includes arguments with friends and family, or with members of the community. You may find empathy and good listening skills play an important role in speaking to an acquaintance or someone you've just met in a variety of situations. Friendships and relationships built around strong emotional intelligence are a good way to begin the connection as well. There are many ways in which attributes of EQ skills can be put into practice to improve your relationship with other people.

The Importance of Empathy and How it Can Foster Deeper Relationships for Personal and Professional Benefit

One of the key components of emotional intelligence is empathy. It is a vastly misunderstood term that can easily be mistaken for sympathy. Sympathy is when we feel sad for someone else's circumstances. This is often expressed as "I feel sorry for you," along with a display of sorrow or pity for them. Empathy, on the other hand, is when you place yourself in the other person's situation and strive to experience or genuinely feel for what they are going through. Expressing empathy means to say, "I feel for what you're going through" or "I understand that must be frustrating or difficult" instead of saying, "I'm sorry to hear what you are going through." It's often easier to show sympathy than empathy, which requires understanding more fully what the other person is experiencing. This may be a challenge if their situation is unfamiliar to us, and in this case, saying "I understand" may not fully capture how you relate to them. Instead, make an effort of trying to empathize by saying, "I can only imagine how difficult this must be" or "You must be going through so much right now." If you are in the position to help, ask first, as what you have to offer may not be what they need at the time.

How can empathy be put into practice? Once you understand how to identify with people and identify with their plight or situation, the focus shifts from an offer of assistance to finding a mutual benefit that is shared with them. In this way, you are with them and working as a team to resolve a matter or strive towards a goal. The following examples highlight how sympathy and empathy differ by showing how effective developing empathy increases the level of emotional intelligence as well.

Scenario 1: Loss of Employment

Angela was devastated after losing her job, and while her employer offered six months of severance pay and continued benefits, she was concerned that the next employment opportunity would not be as lucrative, nor pay the bills. Taking a proactive approach, Angela visited an employment agency and made an appointment with a human resources specialist to update her resume, cover letter, and find a good job. She was scheduled to meet Rick, who was experienced in finding lots of employment for people of all backgrounds and education. He was confident that Angela's skills would land her a good position within just a few months.

Before the meeting, Angela confided in a few close friends and family about her situation. They all offered their support in the form of reassurance that she would find a new job soon, and while she appreciated the comments, they didn't resonate with her as empathetic. In some conversations, phrases like "it can happen to anyone" or "be grateful you have a severance package for six months," which only made her feel worse and minimized her circumstances. She was hoping that her meeting with Rick would pave the way for a better job. Upon arriving at the building to meet with him, Angela was nervous and embarrassed, since she had worked in a professional industry as a retail manager and didn't expect to feel this way.

Rick knew how to handle clients from a wide range of professions and relate to their various situations. Previously, he had been unemployed and understood how difficult it was to re-establish a career and move forward. When clients met with him, Rick needed to instill confidence in his recruitment abilities and knowledge of his field. When he began this position ten years ago, he used sympathy to identify with individuals. Initially, this seemed like a good idea until he realized that it only created a wedge or division. By making statements such as "I'm sorry for your situation" or "it must be a challenging time for you right now," some individuals would respond with "you don't know how I feel" and mentioned how he simply didn't understand them. Furthermore, some clients viewed Rick in a position of privilege or good fortune because he had a job that not only paid well; they also viewed him as making money off their misfortunes. In some scenarios, this would cause some people to feel animosity towards Rick. How could he improve his relationship with clients and display his genuine concern?

Rick understood the basics of empathy, though it wasn't until his employer hosted a seminar at work about the importance of emotional intelligence that it became more vital to put it into practice. Following the meeting, Rick noticed how his communication skills were often one-sided and placed a lot of pressure on his clients to provide as much information to improve their chances. He also focused a lot on his talents and accomplishments to gain their acceptance, though often this created more division, as they simply wanted straight-forward advice and more support than pressure to prove their worthiness of gainful employment. They had already chosen him for his expertise, and therefore the confidence in his ability was already established. Rick wanted to position himself in other people's positions and view their circumstances from their perspective, along with improving his listening skills. Learning a few techniques to strengthen his relationship with people would begin with Angela, his next client.

When Angela arrived, Rick noticed she was visibly nervous, but polite and easy to talk to. Immediately, he calmed her by making a light joke and smiling. This introduction relaxed Angela, and she was quickly able to discuss her situation and ask what Rick could do for her. Before diving into his credentials and details of what he could do, Rick decided to use a different approach: he empathized with Angela and listened to her intently, nodding and acknowledging her frustration with searching for work. "I know how you feel because I've been in your shoes," he expressed, which gave her a sense that he understood her. There was no sense of division, as Angela didn't view Rick on the opposite side of the scenario, but rather, he was mutually working with her on the same side. This encouraged her to make a strong effort in working with Rick, as he had been in the same dilemma and knew the job market well. First, he asked her to focus on developing a marketable resume and cover letter, then assess her current skill set. There was a chance that taking a course or seminar could boost her chances of improving employability, which helped direct Angela in a new direction. Second, Rick asked if she was open to working in other fields related to retail because she had many transferable skills that can translate well in the financial sector. Angela was pleasantly surprised by her options and realized that not only could she find gainful work, but there was a good chance she could earn much more as well.

Rick demonstrated that he was "on her side," and Angela truly felt this because he viewed the situation from her perspective and considered how he would tackle the job hunt journey. As a result of his eagerness and enthusiasm to direct Angela towards success, she was agreeable to his suggestions about taking at least one new course and making drastic changes to the structure of her resume.

Assessment of Scenario 1

Rick was good at his profession and knew he could find virtually anyone a good job if they were willing to work with him. Unfortunately, not everyone was as cooperative and couldn't relate to Rick because he appeared to be very different from them: they were unemployed and, in some cases, lacking financial support, while he worked in a profession that provided a decent salary and benefits. Once Rick curated his approach to meet people on their terms and relate his misfortunes too, people felt understood and as if they were on the same team as Rick. He was there for them and would work to secure them employment as if it was for himself. This approach improved his clients' satisfaction greatly, as well as their chances of success because they were more engaged in the process.

Scenario 2: Classroom Conflict
Jen was a teacher for ten years and took pride in working with many different people and students. She taught regular classes in high school and volunteered as an art instructor at a local community center for both adults and teenagers. Most students in the art class were eager to learn painting, sketching, and other forms of visual art introduced by Jen. On occasion, one or two students would exhibit a difficult personality, usually, because they were often judged for social-economical or other reasons that put them on the defensive. Jen was accepting of everyone, and most people felt this, though a few individuals considered her to be "stuck up" or rude because she was often quiet or slow to respond when someone would ask her a question. Most people didn't know that Jen suffered from hearing loss in one ear, and while she would wear a hearing device to assist, she did experience difficulty understanding sometimes. This led to occasional misunderstanding.

One student, Michaela, was confrontational towards Jen. She never expressed a reason for acting this way, though rumors surfaced that Jen wasn't as engaged with everyone equally. As patient as Jen was most of the time, Michaela challenged her. She would argue about the available paint supplies and often complain that there were never enough canvas options to choose from. Jen tried to appease her by looking for extra items in the storage room, though Michaela was never satisfied and often left the studio early. Sometimes, she was quiet and wouldn't say much, though Michaela's body language indicated discontentment. Jen wanted to make peace somehow, but there was no resolution in sight. Most of the students and faculty were aware of Michaela's difficult behavior and didn't know how to respond. One day, during an unexpected incident of explosive anger, Jen had enough and recommended to the school that Michaela be banned from returning. This was mutually agreed upon, and the faculty unanimously agreed. The following week, Michaela has promptly turned away from the front door to the community center.

In the weeks following this decision, Jen often thought about Michaela and why she was often hostile. She also noted how quiet she was at times, though never seemed to be happy. What would be the cause? Through a few conversations with long-term faculty, it was discovered that Michaela had a history of living in an abusive relationship and struggled with addiction. Her situation was volatile because from one day to the next, her living situation changed. She would leave the relationship, only to return, and repeat, along with numerous attempts to focus on treatment for addiction. A clear picture emerged about Michaela. Jen still agreed with the decision to prohibit her from attending art class, though wished there had been something more that could have been done before the situation escalated. Shortly thereafter, Jen ran into Michaela by chance in a grocery store, which was awkward, but instead of ignoring her, she asked how she was. Michaela initially dismissed her inquiry, but then changed her mind when she noticed the genuine concern on Jen's face. This non-verbal cue made an impact on Michaela because, despite her feelings towards her, a real concern and empathy were showing.

Jen took advantage of the opportunity to apologize about the situation, then found out more about Michaela's circumstances over coffee, then lunch, as both became more familiar. Jen didn't have much in common with Michaela, but she did relate to one thing they had in common: the power of art and its ability to help with the healing process. She offered some references of support and offered to speak with the faculty of the arts program to allow Michaela to return. While Jen was eager to help, Michaela apologized in return for her behavior and wasn't sure if she would be allowed to attend class anymore. Jen empathized with her by explaining how artistic expression helped her through difficult times, and that she would make a priority of offering Michaela a spot in an upcoming class for watercolor painting, which she accepted.

Assessment of Scenario 2

Initially, Jen didn't use much empathy in dealing with Michaela, which only caused more conflict when her behavior escalated. The friction between them escalated because each of them had a misunderstanding about the other: they had both made assumptions that were neither fair nor correct. Despite Jen's attempts to demonstrate patience and tolerance, Michaela's behavior intensified because she had nowhere to vent her frustration and no one to confide in about her challenges. When Jen unveiled the true nature of Michaela's struggles, she didn't have much to share in common except for art and their mutual love for it. Through this mutual understanding, Jen offered Michaela a second chance, but not as a faculty member or art teacher, but as a flow artist who could comprehend the importance of art and its ability to heal and improve life. Jen also improved her listening skills by actively engaging with Michaela and taking into consideration options that she could provide or offer as a way to help.

Scenario 3: Making it Personal

Sandra was interested in dating Greg, who asked her on a date shortly after they became familiar with each other in a local store. While Sandra wasn't keen on getting serious about a relationship too soon, she was willing to give Greg a try since he was charming and had a great sense of humor. He seemed to be a good fit because they shared a lot of the same things in common, from the love of the outdoors to music and film. During the first month of dating, Sandra was aware that Greg had a turbulent relationship, and while she didn't know much about his past, she didn't want to pry. On one occasion, Greg became very emotional, sensing that he was falling heavily for Sandra, and wanted to propose marriage. He blurted out a lot of kinds, heart-warming comments, though Sandra felt it was too soon. She wanted to say no, but instead, asked him to give her time to think it over. This seemed to go well, and Greg seemed hopeful about Sandra's response.

As they continued to date, Sandra sensed an urgency in Greg. He seemed troubled that she wouldn't commit to marriage and explained that while he understood if she needed more time, he wanted to know in advance if there were a chance they would become an official couple in the future. Sandra assured them that they were a couple already and that she would let him know when she was ready. This improved Greg's mood, though as time went on, he grew impatient and would start reacting with frustration and unpredictable comments that startled Sandra. While he was a kind and good-intentioned person, Sandra decided a bit of distance was a good idea. She wanted to explain how Greg's mood changes were difficult to handle, and when she did, he didn't take it well. They ended up taking a temporary split to reconsider their relationship, and Sandra wondered what she could have done differently to help Greg understand. After a month apart, Sandra met with Greg and explained that while she enjoyed being with him, she couldn't handle the constant feeling of pressure to get married or make a commitment. She further mentioned, and understood, that as a result of his previous relationship, there must have been issues with commitment, which worried Greg. He didn't want to invest his time and effort with someone who didn't take him seriously. When Sandra addressed Greg's concerns, he felt immediately relieved. He wanted to know what held Sandra back from a full commitment. She explained that there were career goals that took priority over the next two years, and following this, she would consider the possibility of marriage. While their meeting didn't completely resolve all their conflicts, they had a better understanding of each other and whether they would be a good match in the long term. They mutually decided to give themselves more time to figure it out.

Assessment of Scenario 3
The relationship between Greg and Sandra was positive from the start, and while they communicated a lot, they failed to understand each other's emotions and cues that there was something more at play. For example, Sandra noticed Greg was keen on committing, and initially found this to be admirable, though, after a while, it consumed their

relationship to the point of discomfort. It wasn't until she picked up on cues from his previous experience of dating someone else who failed to take their relationship seriously that she understood the reason for his behavior. On the other hand, Sandra failed to divulge her reasons for putting off the commitment, and instead, led Greg to believe she would give him a more definitive answer, only to avoid the conversation completely. This led to a breakdown in communication and misunderstandings that created frustration and anger between the couple. Greg secretly wondered if Sandra cared for him at all, and she constantly thought about him pushing her towards a final decision about marriage, even though she didn't see this happening shortly, if at all.

Once both Greg and Sandra noticed each other's insecurities and the emotions behind them, they were able to communicate more effectively. Also, they were able to control their behavior better, not just because they made each other aware of the other's impact on them, but they knew more about their options. Greg no longer took Sandra's delay in commitment seriously because it wasn't personal towards him. She developed strong feelings towards him, though he also valued her personal and professional goals, which he understood and respected. Sandra's realization about Greg's past relationship and his strong belief in commitment helped her to understand why he needed that reassurance that she wasn't simply avoiding him but wanted to pursue other goals before settling down.

In all three of the above scenarios, emotional intelligence plays a key role in developing a relationship, whether it's professional, personal, or involves more than one person, such as a community setting. Taking a moment to view a situation from another person's perspective is a powerful and effective way to communicate with them. This technique lets them know that you are willing to try understanding where they are coming from, even if you can't relate from personal experience. Instead of saying, "I understand what you're going through," you could state, "I can only imagine how difficult your situation must be. Let me try to help" or "You must be going through a lot right now, and I can't imagine what that must be like. What can I do?" Show that you want to relate to them, even if the individual is from a different background and may not have a lot in common. There is almost always one item of interest, usually something positive that you can find that connects you with someone, whether it's the same taste in music, film, or sports, for example.

The "Dark" Side of Emotional Intelligence and What You Need to Know

Emotional intelligence is one of the most positive attributes and skill sets you can have in life. Once you develop the ability to understand, self-manage, and articulate other people's emotions, you can relate and communicate with them on a much stronger and personal level. At first glance, EQ appears flawless, and a means to improve our ability to fully understand and care for one another, whether we know someone on a limited basis or more intimately. There is a dark side to emotional intelligence when it is used for manipulative purposes. While the main purpose of EQ is to enhance your connection with other people, it can also become a source of persuasion. Imagine having the ability to hide your true feelings while recognizing genuine emotions in other people, then having the skills to manipulate them based on this knowledge. This situation can give people the advantage because they are aware of their skills and will use them in their own best interests.

Sales professionals and corporate (and political) campaigns will use the same techniques. Only instead of using EQ to secure a stronger understanding and empathy, they use this ability to "read" your emotions to create fear and motivate action based on your worst fears, worries, which in turn, fuel someone else's best interests. While it is important to be aware of these tactics, learning more about the importance of EQ can guard you against these attempts of manipulation. If you know how these techniques can be used against you, you'll notice the rise of fear and uncertainty when you see a specific ad or campaign that aims to achieve this goal. So, while emotional intelligence can have a "darker" side that we may experience, developing the very same skills can give you the advantage to recognize and avoid this pitfall as well.

We are all prone to emotional bias, whether we recognize it or not. When we decide life, it may seem logical at the time, though often there is an emotional component. Consider the following situation and how personal experience and impact on our emotional state can affect a decision-making process:

Edwin enjoyed working as a consultant for a printing firm for five years, though the constant turnover of employees and loss of morale between staff and management was becoming an exhausting experience. A job he once loved and took great pride in became a dreadful place to work. Since he needed the money, he continued working in the firm, though he knew the best option for happiness was to find a better position in another company or organization. After more than five years, Edwin decided to attend a seminar on starting your own business, and become excited about the prospect of working independently, possibly as a consultant between more than one company. During the meeting, he noticed an emotional charge within the audience and a very charismatic group of speakers who were skilled at motivating everyone. This was an experience that Edwin found compelling. As a result of this event, Edwin purchased a few books to read and study for a better way in life.

Following the event, Edwin felt a renewed sense of confidence and decided to announce his resignation. Much to his boss' surprise, Edwin had no job prospects because he was certain that upon leaving the firm, he would find new contracts soon. Despite this, some of his friends and colleagues advised him to take important steps to protect his career and find an alternative employment option first. Edwin was determined that he could make his plan work and abruptly left after two weeks' of notice. In the month that followed, Edwin was "pumped" from the seminar and attended two more meetings that encouraged self-employment, and also offered a direct sales campaign, which Edwin wasn't aware of initially. He initially dismissed the idea, since he wanted to pursue his career path, though, after three weeks without solid leads, he felt compelled to give it a try. As he delved into the world of direct sales, he soon uncovered a pyramid-scheme that disappointed him greatly. When he considered the idea of returning to his previous position, despite his reluctance to do so, he found that the firm was on the verge of going out of business and would close soon. Had he stayed a month or more longer, he would have met the same fate in losing his job, though he would also receive benefits and a severance package, unlike quitting, which meant Edwin would be out of luck.

Edwin decided to learn from this experience because while he wanted a better career path and job prospects, he took an impulsive turn that led him into near financial devastation. Fortunately, he was able to find a new job that wasn't exactly what he wanted, though it paid well and provided a positive environment. When reflecting on his previous decision to leave his job, he realized how quickly he made a choice to leave, which was heavily influenced by the emotionally charged seminar, which used his fears of not achieving his full potential against him. In doing this, Edwin not only caved into buying materials and books that did nothing for his current situation, but he also lacked a solid plan and alternative to move into a new direction. Without this plan in place, his resignation was based purely on emotions. In this way, emotional intelligence was lacking in Edwin's overall plan, while the EQ skills employed by the speakers at the seminar were used to foster a sense of urgency and "act now or miss out" mentality to gain sales and a stronger following among the audience.

In considering the above example, Edwin was heavily influenced at the seminar, shortly after he grew frustrated and unhappy with his work environment and prospects on the job. The lack of morale and constant changing of staff led him to feel unwanted and underappreciated at work. Instead of recognizing these feelings and learning to cope with them until finding another employment opportunity, Edwin was drawn to any opportunity, even an unrealistic one, at that moment, because it was a distraction from his life and offered a sense of hope for the future. In any other circumstance, Edwin wouldn't have attended the seminar, which was disguised as a sure-fire way to achieve success, and instead, it was a marketing scheme aimed at people in his situation. The speakers and organizers of the event were skilled at using emotional intelligence to their advantage by attracting people who felt desperate and eager to make money on their terms and were willing to try anything new to achieve this goal.

Once Edwin became aware of the tactics used at the seminar, and how he fell prey to them, he later understood how important it was to recognize his emotional state and feelings before other people could take advantage of them. In this moment of "weakness," he was more likely to follow and listen, instead of a question and assess the situation, and for this reason, Edwin decided never to make hasty decisions again, especially concerning his employment.

How can you recognize when emotional intelligence can be used against you? Firstly, it's important to realize that learning EQ skills will guard you against the very tactics that can take advantage of you. You'll need to recognize when you are most vulnerable to influence and distinguish between whether someone is genuinely helpful and altruistic or simply targeting you because of circumstance. This is a tactic used in politics often, where one party or candidate becomes aware of society's concerns and fears. This may be the result of the current political party in power, and how they may have mishandled certain situations, including finances, changes in legislation, or a lack of leadership. In these instances, the public may become divisive, which makes it easier to conquer or influence the way indecisive people feel about voting for someone different. Furthermore, by instilling fear or concern about a specific person or party, the ability to emotionally control and direct someone or a group towards a favorable decision is more likely. People are often led by their emotions and can make impulsive choices based on them.

Once you know your emotions well, you will notice this tactic immediately and can guard against it. This will give you a good sense of what to look for when you choose life:
- Have you weighed all the pros and cons associated with a specific decision, or is it a choice you are willing to make based on emotion alone?
- What are the real advantages of deciding for or against a cause or situation?
- Does the group or individual(s) influence your decision to have something to gain from it? When you see them in person, on television, or online, do they evoke an emotional response from you?

These questions are just a sample of what you should ask yourself before finalizing a decision. As you encounter the impact of various influences and persuasion, and in some cases, manipulation, consider this when you see what choice(s) you are being presented with. Often, manipulation of your emotions will appear as an "all or nothing" tactic. This works in sales too, as a prospective client is offered to buy a complete package or product, or "miss out" by walking away. This technique tries to draw out a sense of longing for a product or service by making it exclusive and more special than anywhere else, thus coaxing the customer to sign a contract and spend, even if he/she doesn't have the budget to afford it.

In less extreme cases, manipulation of emotions can happen in personal and work relationships, where one person uses guilt or a sense of obligation to influence you to do something for them. This often occurs in relationships where one person, usually the influencer, has a position of authority over the other. However, this can work in reverse where the employee appeals to his/her boss with compliments or a sense of loyalty to get something they want. Emotional intelligence isn't always present in these cases, as many tactics of manipulation use charisma and fear-mongering, though once a person knows how to read the emotional response and identify feelings in other people, including non-verbal cues, this can lead them to an advantageous position where they can use this to their advantage.

How to Guard Against Tactics Used Against You By Developing Emotional Intelligence

The same set of skills used to work against you can also work in your favor and give you the advantage in the long run. Once you notice how your emotions can be used against you, you'll have a better sense of how to react and gauge your behaviors based on how you feel. For example, instead of showing shock and amazement at a sales pitch, you might remain calm or slightly inquisitive, not allowing the other person to gauge your true feelings. On the other hand, you'll be able to notice whether or not their intentions are positive or mutually beneficial, or whether they are simply looking to gain something from you.

- How well is your decision making made independently, based on your assessment, versus how well someone else convinced you to vote and decide a certain way?
- Are there any circumstances in your life, such as a loss of a job, a tragedy, or a vulnerable situation that may cause you to feel more compelled to make a decision you could regret later?
- Does the thought of making one choice over another evoke a strong emotional response? Is this the primary reason you are leaning towards a decision?

- How much influence does someone have over you, and do you feel the need to answer to them? If so, are they altruistic in their reason, or do they have something to gain from your choice?

When you assess a situation, always consider the emotional component involved. For many situations that may not seem to be emotionally charged or involved feelings, we tend to ignore how obvious we react and decide in many scenarios, due to personal thoughts and feelings under certain circumstances. If you consider yourself to be in a vulnerable situation financially, emotionally, or otherwise, be wary of anyone offering a quick and easy solution. There is usually a price attached that isn't affordable, nor is it beneficial in the long term. Understanding how emotional intelligence can work as a means to persuade or manipulate doesn't mean it should be avoided. On the contrary, EQ skills are highly valuable and can serve to help you gain a lot out of work and personal relationships by connecting better with people. The ultimate reason for learning and applying EQ lies in the true intention and ethics that you apply when exercising these skills.

The Case Against Emotional Intelligence: Are There More Disadvantages Than Advantages?

The popularity and widespread use of EQ skills and their benefits at work and home can be an excellent way to foster and improve relationships with people, though it can also be used against someone as well, as discussed earlier in this book. As people become more accustomed to a workplace or lifestyle where the attributes of emotional intelligence are well respected and useful, they may feign empathy or pretend to listen intently to a conversation, even when they do not wish to develop any relationship at all. In these types of situations, emotional intelligence can be used to deceive and convince others there is altruism when there is really an opportunity to be exploited. It is these types of instances that question the overall validity of EQ and how impactful it is in everyday life:

- If a person says they care about you and your situation, are they sincere, or do they have something to gain by making this statement?
- Is the person trustworthy in general, or do they need to convince you they can be relied upon?
- Does an individual have a strong influence or impact on how you feel everything you are around them? Does this level of charisma seem genuine, or does it always end with you doing something for them, whether it is in your best interest or not?

There are potential side effects or a downside of emotional intelligence, not only in the people who develop these skills but the outcome of employing them as well. While studies have indicated people with strong EQ skills perform well in social environments and excel in customer service and client relations roles, there are other characteristics that indicate higher instances of depression, stress, and anxiety among the same population. People who ranked high in emotional intelligence were also more likely to cave into social pressure, even when they felt the decision to do so was against their best interest or against the organization or company. This is akin to a student making drastic changes to their appearance and habits to "fit into" the mainstream at school and avoid conflict. While EQ skills highlight the need to negotiate and find a balance between various points of view, some people are emotionally charged and feel less pressure if they simply change their perspective and agree with the other side, even if they do not authentically feel this way.

Leadership requires assertiveness and a balanced, disciplined approach to how people and situations are handled. In a perfect environment, leadership can maintain complete balance and continue towards a goal that benefits their community or company, where everyone is compliant and in agreement. Realistically, leaders must contend with dissension and disagreements often, which means they must negotiate, and in some cases, compromise with others. Emotional intelligence plays a role in this process because it is advantageous to connect and relate to other people during a negotiation. They are more likely to see your point of view if you respect or acknowledge theirs. On the other hand, some people with strong EQ skills can exhibit a high degree of empathy that can cloud their judgment, specifically where a difficult decision must be made, or an individual is dismissed or laid off. Delivering difficult news to a group of people can be especially challenging when the spokesperson is hesitant to make the announcement and may respond with their own emotions during this time. In these cases, a high degree of empathy can work against you and even compromise the ability to function as a leader or negotiator. If another individual notices this trend, they can take full advantage by using emotionally inducing language and subject matter to invoke a reaction that could work more in their favor.

Manipulating people with strong emotions and empathy is common. Some people may assert that certain companies or organizations hire people with high EQ scores because they are easy to manage and control, especially in a large corporation. While this is debatable, some organizations may consider an emotionally intelligent person more compliant and less prone to dissension than someone without the same skill set. An individual in a leadership position may also be susceptible to persuasion and lose their footing within an organization as a result. While these are extreme examples and not always realistic, the emotional volatility of a person can have a major impact on many situations, especially if they rise to a position of authority and responsibility. Imagine having the pressure of having more to oversee and decide on, and its impact on the level of stress on someone who is more empathetic or emotionally intelligent.

As people increase their emotional intelligence, they don't always become more emotional themselves, but rather, learn to understand, interpret their feelings and those of others. This process allows them to magnify and examine the way other people react and behave as a result of their feelings, which stem from various experiences and events. In this way, emotionally intelligent people are better equipped to appreciate and understand why a person may have a specific feeling and can identify with them just enough to work from this perspective. There is a fine line between deeply understanding the underlying cause of the emotion and connecting with someone through empathy than personally feeling the same emotion and allowing this experience to skew your judgment for or against a situation as a result.

There are many perceptions about EQ and how it works, which explains the source of criticism. While there are some notable drawbacks, the overall benefit of connecting with people on a more personable level is advantageous. Many people with EQ skills are able to control the impact of emotions from other people, as well as their own, though this varies from one individual to the next. In some situations, a person with emotional intelligence may display signs of hypersensitivity, where they are acutely tuned in to another person's behavior and actions as a result of their emotions and may become affected by it. In many fields of work, employees or specialists in social or community work learn to guard their own feelings and observe others from a different perspective. This practice allows a person with empathy to identify with another individual, though not to the point where they become emotionally involved with them. In doing so, they can keep a professional distance while addressing the needs of a client. In the case of a personal relationship, the distance factor may be required when there are implications in getting too involved in a conflict, as boundaries can be blurred, or lines crossed in the process.

Responsibility and Emotional Intelligence

Every professional or individual with high emotional intelligence knows the ramifications of these skills and how to use them. While the ability to identify and empathize with a group or individual is an amazing way to understand and resolve conflict, it can open another level of responsibility. This factor especially applies to people who are in a leadership position and need to use their level of expertise as a way to make an appropriate decision. What happens if the decision they need to make benefits the individual(s) involved, but goes against the interests of an organization or a community? Consider a situation where a person must keep all information from their client as confidential, such as an attorney. Then they are faced with a dilemma where they must retain the information they learn from an individual or disclose it to prevent further damage from occurring. While there are laws in place that provide guidelines on what information must and cannot be revealed, there can be a fine line in more personal situations when a deep sense of empathy is experienced. Consider the following example to illustrate this dilemma:

Alice was married for ten years to her partner, Mike, and they had two children. Alice was the co-owner of a floral shop with her best friend, Kyra. Both Kyra and Alice enjoyed strong friendship and partnership in business that lasted over fifteen years, and they entrusted most (if not all) of their secrets to one another. On one afternoon, Kyra accidentally notices Mike with someone else, and it is clear that he is having an extramarital affair. Shocked, she considers approaching him, though decides to confront Mike may not go well, as he may threaten her not to disclose her discovery to his wife, Alice. After all, they have two young kids, and this would place the couple in a difficult situation. Alice deserved to know, Kyra thought, though she weighed the implications of the situation by using empathy and trying to view the situation from both Mika and Alice's perspective:

If Mike knew Kyra was aware of his indiscretion, he wouldn't trust her and may use blackmail to ensure she doesn't say anything to Alice. While this may or may not happen, Kyra was aware that divulging a highly secretive situation to Mike could inflate an emotional response that would be difficult to handle, and it is a decision that could not be reversed. There was also the implication of the business that she owned with his wife, Alice. If Alice decided to pursue a divorce, this could have a dire impact on the flower shop. Mike could plead with Kyra to keep the secret in exchange for a favor, though this is not something she wanted to entertain as a possibility.

Alice, on the other hand, could react with anger and sadness. If she suspected that Kyra withheld the information from her, there could be a loss of trust and a breakdown in the business partnership and friendship. Keeping the news of the affair secret would allow everything to continue as usual, without any implications.

The easiest part of the scenario was neither Mike nor Alice nor anyone else knew Kyra was aware of the indiscretion. As a result, she could continue undetected, as if nothing happened. If Alice happened to discover the affair, Kyra could easily avoid the situation because she could simply pretend not to know. She could offer an empathetic approach to the devastating news and listen to Alice. This would be the best option under the circumstance and allow the friendship and partnership to continue.

There are various opinions about whether Kyra should divulge her discovery or not. From an ethical standpoint, some could argue that she has a duty to report the indiscretion to her friend, while for the same reason, not telling her would be the kind approach, as Mike may never be caught and the affair may continue uninterrupted, or simply stop on its own. Emotional intelligence plays a role in determining how each person's role in the scenario would be impacted by either knowing what Kyra discovered in comparison to how their lives would continue without her disclosing. Essentially, the decision becomes a matter of which direction would be the least painful, and Kyra must consider the impact of a decision either way.

In situations where it is legally required to either disclose or withhold certain information, the decision is clear, though, in personal situations or scenarios where all parties involved, their behavior and emotional reaction must be considered, there is a level of EQ skills needed to assess the situation carefully. In Kyra's dilemma, there is no perfect approach, but the least painful path was to leave what she witnessed as is and never speak of it to Mike or Alice. This meant that Kyra would have to deal with her own feelings about Mike and struggle with knowing more than both. On the other hand, divulging the affair would cause more damage, and Kyra was not prepared to deal with a business partner who may be facing divorce, which could have a negative impact on sales and the financial success of their partnership. Kyra chose the option that would benefit everyone most, including herself.

Emotional Intelligence as a Form of Motivation

Making a connection with a group of people is a profound and highly effective way to encourage and empower others. This is a strong skill for motivational speakers and people who hold a prestigious status in a community or in a greater sense, like a celebrity. While EQ can be misused to manipulate and gain influence over other people, it is generally well-received as a powerful way to improve a person's morale or confidence when they face a challenging role within an organization or in life. Have you worked for a boss who always knew how to say the right words when you became doubtful in your ability to achieve your target or goal? Has anyone provided a source of comfort by giving you the moral support needed during a difficult time? A person with the ability to make you feel empowered and able usually has a strong EQ sense and may know what it's like to be in your position. They may have experienced some of the same doubts and emotions that you did and know what to say to improve your outlook. Some individuals are talented at motivating others; they often offer advice and stories of their own to help you relate to their past situations and needs.

When you encounter someone with EQ skills, how does it impact your ability to develop your own sense of confidence and relationships with others? While motivation is a key way to improve the performance of employees and enhance relationships, a person with emotional intelligence must be convincing and sincere in their motives for their audience to reap the rewards of their advice and direction in life. Many people are satisfied with having someone take control of their lives and "fix" them, which may seem like a form of admiration and respect. This can also feel like a heavy burden on the person with EQ, who may take their role seriously, though not take on more responsibility than they should. The ultimate goal of motivation is to instill a sense of direction in someone, so they can take greater control of their own destiny, rather than expecting it to be done for them.

Emotional Intelligence = Emotional Wisdom

Considering all components of emotional intelligence, whether it's the advantages, drawbacks, and specific impact of EQ on real-life scenarios, people with a good EQ foundation tend to be wise in many aspects of their professional and personal life. This includes making better decisions concerning money and finances while securing long-term relationships that are mutually beneficial and demonstrating a willingness to become part of the solution. They are the managers who place their employees' and clients' comfort as a priority because they know how much this impacts the success of business and stability within an organization. After making a mistake, a person with good EQ skills is more likely to admit to their fault and learn from the error, instead of shifting blame to another person or minimizing the outcome. This is a major reason why most work relationships function well with an emotionally intelligent leader at the helm. They know operations will be handled in fairness and with the best interest of the company in mind.

How can attaining emotional intelligence lead to wisdom? When we learn to observe and understand human nature, we have a better grasp of why people behave in various ways and how they react. This process begins by understanding ourselves first, and how what we experience and feel impacts our behavior. Emotional self-awareness is one of the first steps in understanding the degree of importance that our feelings have on our actions. Once we can identify our personal connection between emotion and behavior, it becomes easier to recognize it in others. You'll find yourself saying some of these statements internally, as you observe what other people experience:

- "If I experienced what he/she is going through, I would be angry and have difficulty responding with a clear mind for a while."
- "They went through a tragic event, and if I did the same, I'd want some time away from other people for a while."
- "I can sense the tension in the boardroom and notice how a couple of people are using restraint before making a statement. I will wait to see how this continues and offer a solution or suggestion when the time is right."

Sometimes, while it may seem like a situation calls for immediate action, it is what we say (or don't say) that makes a significant difference. As we grow older, we tend to balance our emotional response more carefully. For this reason, some companies prefer to hire some mature, older individuals to work with young, ambitious staff as a form of mentoring. This also transfers into our personal relationships, and what we may have responded to prematurely and without thinking in youth may be a point of pondering or consideration later in life. There are other aspects of emotional intelligence that help increase and strengthen the level of wisdom over time:

- A stronger sense of who we are and what makes us "tick." This is how we can find common ground with other people who may seem different than us at first glance.
- We learn to appreciate diversity in society and focus more on strengths than weaknesses. Collectively, we'll have a better idea of which individuals contribute more than others, and how a variety of skills can build a strong team.
- Connecting with other people means we have better relationships with more focus on quality instead of quantity. We are likely to

have fewer friendships with deeper meaning and connection than many superficial friends without the same bond.
- We avoid conflict, though when facing confrontation, finding common ground and managing the situation takes precedence over being correct or having the last word or final say. The more we argue and assert correctness, the less the other person hears what we have to say, and we also fail to listen to their opinion as well as actively.
- There is greater compassion and concern for other people, and placing others' well being as a priority. Selflessness is also associated with empathy and emotional intelligence, which means we take in a greater view of our overall impact on other people and the greater community.

Another aspect of emotional intelligence is the ability to look forward and focus on the future, without pondering on the past or worrying about mistakes. Being in the present is an important aspect of staying relevant while working towards future milestones and goals. There will always be setbacks and issues in life, though focusing on the opportunities available and stressing these points to other people who need motivation is a great way to improve your connection with them. Giving people a sense of importance and purpose by connecting with them shows that we are thinking beyond our own needs. This approach shows compassion and cares for other people, who will work more cooperatively towards a shared goal or target.

The Term Emotional Intelligence and How it Has Evolved

Why call it emotional intelligence? Our ability to recognize emotions in other people and identify them is key to survival. Whether a person shows anger or sadness can significantly affect how we react, and it can also protect us from making the wrong move. Our emotions have evolved, in part, for this purpose: to understand our feelings and others, so that we can communicate more effectively and adapt according to a changing situation. A specific reaction can be interpreted as a threat in some situations, such as frustration or anger, though fear or surprise can startle or impair someone momentarily and give someone else the advantage in that situation. Our cognitive ability to understand emotions and how they work has continued to develop, and emotional intelligence aims to capture this process in a way that indicates how important it is to understand and read people.

Human intelligence has been studied for centuries, though the emotional component of intelligence wasn't a focus until much later, until the 1930s. EQ became a major research subject in the 1990s, which found its way into the workplace. Before then, social intelligence was a field of study that focused on how people got along with each other. It encompassed moods, attitudes, and feelings between individuals and groups, and how emotions played a role in the process of socialization. It was noted how some people had a predisposition to get along with other people, even those with a difference of opinion, than others.

From almost a century ago to the 1990s, social intelligence became EQ, which developed into a popular new trend of study for employers, sociologists, and anyone interested in understanding a person's skill level at understanding emotions and building social skills. There were common attributes associated with people who demonstrated strong social skills, including:

- The ability to socialize well with other people and find common ground
- Display empathy and awareness of what other people are going through
- Handling the way other people express their emotions and the behaviors that result from them.
- Understanding their own emotions and how this impacts behavior and action

While EQ skill testing is used widely today, it has evolved into a more specific set of questions and criteria for various roles at work. Most people know about emotional intelligence on an informal level. They may assess individuals they know in their personal life to determine if they are a good fit. If a person is self-aware and open to negotiating with an open mind, this makes a positive impression. As more people learn the fundamentals of emotional intelligence, it not only helps them to improve personal EQ skills, it will give them the tools to notice these attributes in other people. Emotional intelligence is no longer just a topic of research or a specific field of study for analysis. It's a common household term that most people understand and consider a valuable skill.

CHAPTER 6
Myths Vs. Facts About Eq

Common Misperceptions About Emotional Intelligence and the Reality of This Valuable Skill Set

There are many misperceptions about emotional intelligence and the importance of possessing and developing these skills in life. While many people, including employers and experts in psychology, see empathy as a win-win for many aspects in life, there are myths and misperceptions about what EQ is all about and its effectiveness. The following myths are commonly stated in response to learning about emotional intelligence.

Myth: Emotional intelligence is not as important as IQ or other skills needed in life and the workplace.

Fact: This myth is a common misperception of what EQ is and its importance. While emotional intelligence cannot replace practical knowledge and expertise in specific fields of employment, it is a vital set of skills to have when dealing with a variety of scenarios on the job. The way we interact with other people and regulate our emotions and actions become an integral part of how we conduct ourselves in business relations and other aspects of our career. While EQ is considered a central part of determining whether someone is fit for a position, this is often a part of a broader scope of credentials and requirements that must also be met or exceeded for consideration.

Myth: Emotional intelligence is not real/does not exist.

Fact: While EQ skills or emotional intelligence is a new concept from the 1990s, there are much older and respected principles that have been around for centuries and beyond. These include principles or widely held beliefs that we should listen before we speak, be slow to anger (or avoid it completely), and not pass judgment. Many of these guidelines have been taught and practiced through both cultural and religious beliefs to improve relationships with other people and regulate our emotions. While EQ is a new concept, the foundation for these skills and developing them have been around for much longer.

Myth: People who react emotionally often or display a strong ability to express how they feel have a high EQ.

Fact: Scoring high in EQ skills doesn't require that you react emotionally or relate to everyone with your response. While some individuals are naturally more inclined to express their feelings outwardly, especially if they are comfortable in doing so. This can work against you and the other person where the emotional response is not regulated. This can result in misunderstandings and may lead to conflict. Empathy, on the other hand, means you place yourself in the other person's situation to gain a better understanding of their plight so that you can respond in kind, but not necessarily with strong emotions. EQ is also about regulating how we speak and what we say, to avoid potential issues arising from misunderstandings.

Myth: EQ is natural once you have it, and there is no need to sharpen your skills once you score well in emotional intelligence.

Fact: While some individuals are naturally prone to scoring high in EQ and developing empathy for others, everyone can benefit from self-reflection and awareness. We are often learning new and important things about people and what they go through, either collectively as a group or as individuals. How we respond to one person in a specific situation may not bode well to another individual going through the same experience.

Myth: People with high EQ skills are the best to take charge and should be considered for leadership roles.

Fact: Emotional intelligence is ideal for anyone, including people in positions of authority or leadership; however, EQ skills can be used to persuade and motivate people against their will and to manipulate. While some people (and organizations) view this as acceptable, depending on their overall goals and sales targets, it can backfire on establishing relationships between people who use EQ against others and those targeted for this purpose. For this reason, using emotional intelligence appropriately and understanding how to use it for, not against, your benefit and others are essential.

Myth: Emotional intelligence is manipulative and doesn't truly serve to help anyone but the person practicing EQ techniques.

Fact: This is an understandable conclusion, considering how EQ skills can be manipulated into controlling how other people see us and how they respond. While EQ can be applied in this way, it has a lot of positive results when we develop strong skills from a young age. Emotional intelligence gives you the ability to determine how you can act or behave appropriately based on another person's emotion, but also by assessing our feelings. Controlling our emotions means we know how and why they occur and how to stop them from having an impact on our behavior and action. This can lead to a more positive outcome, as we are not simply reacting, but taking a moment to reflect on how to communicate appropriately instead. In this way, we are controlling our emotions and the way other people act towards us. However, this is a positive way to build trust and a strong relationship with other people in professional and personal life.

Myth: High EQ is the same as scoring high on IQ

Fact: IQ has always been considered as the primary way for testing intelligence, though it has nothing to do with a person's capacity for empathy or social skills. Is an individual scoring high in IQ may perform numerous complex tasks on the job, including technical procedures associated with their advanced skills, though how do they relate to colleagues? Do they know how to form strong negotiation skills in the same way they can solve advanced math equations? A person with a high IQ may be inept in how they relate to other people socially and might prefer to work alone or independently. For this reason, many employers focus on emotional intelligence and provide testing for prospective new hires to gauge their ability to work well with others and clients as well.

Myth: Charisma is associated with having a good EQ score.

Fact: Charm and charisma are attractive traits and often work to persuade or coax someone. A person with these characteristics can appear to have emotional intelligence because they are friendly and make a positive, strong impression at once. They may appear to empathize with you, though they intend to manipulate and convince you to let your guard down. They don't listen to you in a way that they want to understand or empathize with a mutual benefit. If charisma is applied without empathy, then it can be used as a tool to manipulate another person, convincing them to take a direction or path that they may not otherwise choose.

Myth: There is no real benefit to improving EQ skills in the same way as other skills, such as technical and industry-specific knowledge.

Fact: With more research and studies on the benefits of EQ testing and application in the workplace, the rate of return from improved emotional intelligence is better than expected. While most businesses and clients are looking for capable, hard-working candidates, they also appreciate the ability to relate on a personal level and connect better with people who have strong social skills. An individual with sharp technical skills who cannot relate with others socially will miss out on many opportunities as a result. In many organizations, EQ skill assessment is placed high on the priority of criteria for employment consideration. In business and marketing, this is especially important as how we resonate with people and groups can determine how much of an interest they will take in a product or service. Also, if someone can relate to us on a personable level, this will secure a stronger relationship in the longer term.

Myth: The idea of improving EQ skills is like a therapy session where you get "in touch" with your emotions.

Fact: Initially, many people may feel this way because of the focus on recognizing and identifying emotions and their impact on us and others. Contrary to this myth, EQ is about learning how to recognize and control our actions that stem from emotions, not simply to explore and express them. Once we understand the strength of our emotions and how they impact others through our actions, we can take greater steps to control how we act and communicate. Similarly, EQ skills are also about recognizing emotional states in other people and knowing how and when to respond appropriately.

Myth: Emotional intelligence varies from one gender, culture, or generation to the next

Fact: On the surface, there are differences in how we express our feelings and thoughts, though anyone can develop strong EQ skills at any age. While our upbringing and culture will differ from one individual to the next, the overall ability to curate strong EQ is an advantage that's open to anyone willing to develop them. No one group or person is more likely to develop emotional intelligence than another, as long as they are willing to learn and develop these skills.

Myth: Emotional people tend to score high in EQ skills.

Fact: Just because someone is emotional and comfortable with their feelings doesn't automatically mean they are good at managing how they express them. When a person is emotional, they can seem sympathetic, even display signs of empathy, though it may only be as a result of the moment they are currently experiencing and will disappear once they feel less impacted by an emotional event or situation. Emotional intelligence refers to the ability to recognize when a feeling is present and then decide how to respond to it appropriately. The management of the feeling must be present along with the emotion itself, for EQ to become effective.

Myth: Emotional intelligence is needed, especially for people who exhibit toxic and abusive behavior.

Fact: EQ skill-building is for everyone, even individuals who are already highly skilled in emotional intelligence. While toxic people may seem like prime examples of individuals who will benefit from learning empathy and good listening skills, all people need to develop and improve over time.

Myth: EQ skills are something you have or lack. Some people don't have the capacity to develop emotional intelligence.

Fact: While some individuals are not keen on developing EQ and choose not to work on these skills, anyone can develop emotional intelligence. This begins with becoming mindful of your actions and how they relate to your emotions. Not everyone is aware of this connection, but once you recognize how a specific comment or action towards someone else is rooted in a change in mood or feelings, you have the power to change how you act and what you say. This can make a significant difference in your relationships, often improving them significantly. As long as you have the willingness to learn and adapt, you can learn EQ skills and apply them in many scenarios.

Myth: A shy and introverted person is not likely to develop strong EQ skills.

Fact: On the surface, an individual with a tendency to shy away from social situations may appear to be anti-social, though there can be other factors at work. For example, some people are naturally comfortable on their own, and careful how they approach others, though once they communicate and feel comfortable, they become very empathetic and understanding. Some quiet people tend to observe more than they speak. They assess a situation before they get involved with how to respond. This means they can display a high degree of EQ and know exactly when and how to act and behave. In this way, a more reserved personality is more prone to developing emotional intelligence because they take their time to assess how other people communicate and behave, which often indicates their emotional state. While not everyone shy or hesitant to socialize is automatically high in EQ skills, they have the potential to develop them by their very nature because they take the time to "read" and understand people and the conversation in progress before they respond, which is often given thought beforehand.

Myth: Emotional intelligence cannot be taken seriously, as anyone can fake their ability to empathize.

Fact: For the most part, people will exhibit various levels of emotional intelligence, though only a small percentage act contrary to their true nature where EQ skills are concerned. Tests that assess the level of EQ ability have come a long way from their prototypes. As the value of emotional intelligence is regarded highly in many industries, questionnaires and interviews have been customized to filter through applicants during the recruitment process. Some people empathize naturally, which is often easy to identify. While others can feign their natural ability to care, a professional can often see through this. Emotional intelligence is more than pretending to have empathy and faking a display of care for another person. EQ entails a full range of abilities to understand and react reasonably to how other people behave and understand the true nature of our own emotions.

Myth: Developing emotional intelligence is as easy as "tapping" into your emotions.

Fact: Learning EQ skills is not as easy as it seems, though it can be more natural for some people than others. Most people need time to adjust and develop an understanding of their own emotions before they can assess others. While some people believe they can understand someone else's feelings well, they may not have a good grasp of their own emotions. The ability to connect with your emotional intelligence must be built through the limbic system in the brain. Self-awareness involves more than simply "tapping" into emotions, because we may know a certain way of feeling, but not why or how we should react as a result.

Myth: Children don't have emotional intelligence.

Fact: At a young age, children may not exhibit the level of EQ skills that adults are capable of, though some kids can show signs early in some ways. For example, if a child feels sadness or empathy for a hurt animal or pet, or they are good at listening to a friend who feels upset or emotionally upset, this can make a significant difference in how they develop later. Early development is possible, though, like other aspects of cognitive and emotional skills, some children can indicate a natural tendency to care for others and understand the feelings in other people sooner. Emotional intelligence can be developed in anyone at any age, with enough awareness and practice.

Myth: Once you know emotional intelligence, you're going to have the same skills always.

Fact: While emotional intelligence is an acquired skill set, it needs to be practiced and improved on a regular basis. It is possible to regress, especially when it's not expected to happen. We can become too comfortable in understanding how we feel and the way other people think or express their emotions. It can be easy to think we are well versed in EQ skills once we land the right job and pass an assessment, though our ability to use these can get less effective over time. Maintaining sharp EQ skills means keeping engaged with other people and staying on top of your abilities. Any practice or skill set is only as polished as you make use of them.

CHAPTER 7
Frequently Asked Questions

Question: How do I know whether a job will require that I score highly on an EQ skills test or demonstrate emotional intelligence?

Answer: If an employment opportunity includes a significant role within a community and handling client relations, customer service, or communicating with the public in general, there is a good chance your application and assessment for the job will entail measuring your skills for emotional intelligence. Your potential employer will want you to demonstrate that you can regulate your emotional response and handle difficult situations, even if they don't expect you to encounter any regularly. The EQ test is usually included in the interview and application process and evaluated along with other factors to determine your fitness for the job.

Question: How can I find out if someone has strong EQ or emotional intelligence skills?

Answer: There are some key characteristics you'll notice in people who have a degree of EQ skills. These can be detected even if you don't know them well or within a limited context (at work, in the general community). Attributes of emotional intelligence include having successful leadership qualities and the ability to take charge while listening to other people and working with them effectively. They are often respected and listened to, and in turn, they take the time to become aware of how others feel and act towards them and listen to the concerns of other people so that they can address them fairly and with empathy. People with strong EQ skills tend to be patient and understanding of others and avoid conflict as much as possible, often choosing an amicable way to resolve differences and work towards shared goals. You may know a teacher or professor with these traits or notice them in a local community leader or activist. People with emotional intelligence tend to take on roles with more responsibility and are willing to take on challenging roles to better their community and relationships with other people, either for a variety of reasons.

Question: If a person displays a high level of emotional intelligence, does this mean they lack logic as a result? Does the capitalization or focus on EQ skills in work and personal life take priority over using rationalization and logic in resolving issues?

Answer: This is not accurate, as the presence of emotional intelligence and empathy towards people can play a role alongside making logical decisions and directions for the improvement of a situation. Displaying empathy and exercising good listening skills to understand other people can lead to logical conclusions because we have a better sense of what (and who) we are handling. Regulating our own emotional and behavioral response is also another way that we use thought and logical reasoning over emotion to decide. For example, our awareness that a certain situation or person will trigger an emotional response can signal a lack of control; however, if we are aware of a potential reactionary reply or behavior, we can prepare ahead to avoid any misunderstanding. EQ takes into consideration the importance of regulating how you interact with other people while remaining self-aware during the process. This means more logic, not less, will play a role in improving situations.

Question: Can emotional intelligence be developed in childhood, and how can it be encouraged in children who do not display signs of EQ development at a young age?

Answer: In childhood, emotional development is ongoing, which includes the ability to regulate the expression and understanding of our feelings and emotions. A child will likely react without thinking first, especially if they are young, as they have not yet developed a filter or means to assess their feelings before expressing them. This often results in loud outbursts or temper tantrums in small kids (babies and toddlers), and later, as outbursts and inconsistent expressions in pre-teen and teenage years. Hormonal changes and development also play a role in how we process and understand our emotions. Some children are skilled at resolving issues from a young age, including how to react with restrained emotion. This is often due to observing adults and noticing how they handle various situations through discussions or finding a solution proactively. While feelings are important to recognize, acknowledge, and experience, understanding their purpose. If a child understands the reason why they feel a certain way, this can help them respond to a situation rationally.

Parents or primary caregivers often have the most impact on how children develop emotionally, including their ability to form strong EQ skills. It's important to encourage traits related to emotional intelligence to improve your child's normal development and increase their ability to succeed in life. There are important pitfalls to avoid that many parents and caregivers may not recognize, and sometimes the best intentions can become more harmful than helpful. Consider the following reasons why some children experience difficulties when processing and understanding their emotions:

- When their feelings or thoughts are dismissed as unimportant, this can cause a child to undermine their own emotions or see them as a distraction or nuisance. Emotions are important and need validation, not dismissal. When a child is ignored, they eventually learn to internalize their feelings and avoid expressing them completely.

- In situations where a child is allowed, even encouraged, to express and accept all emotions, this can be valuable, as long as they also learn how to react and respond appropriately. Accepting an emotion is important, though not understanding the full implications on how to self-manage and behave or act as a result can lead to misunderstandings and conflict.
- They are focusing on positive emotions only and ignoring or discouraging any feelings that are associated with negativity. While no one wants to focus on anger, sadness, and other feelings associated with negative emotions, they remain just as valid and should never be ignored or dismissed. When some parents or caregivers punish a child or discourage them from feeling "bad," this can lead to repressed emotions and difficulty with anger management and other challenges later in life.

Generally, the development of emotions in a child varies considerably based on their upbringing, and the values instilled in them about emotions. In certain cultures and societies, the emotional expression may be suppressed, and any sign of feelings are strongly mocked or dismissed. This can have devastating, long-lasting effects on people who are taught to hide their true feelings. For these reasons, children should always be encouraged to recognize and validate their emotions, then find meaningful and constructive ways to express them.

Question: Can a high level of EQ skills guarantee success?
Answer: Developing strong emotional intelligence is vital for many aspects of life, though, like any skill set, there is never a 100% guarantee of success. While many people with good EQ skills are successful, many do not have these qualities, and yet they have found success. On the other hand, emotional intelligence can open the doors to many opportunities that you may not have encountered previously, such as a new job or career prospects, and connections with people in business and personal life. While EQ doesn't guarantee you'll excel in a specific path or direction, it can enhance and improve many aspects of your life in general, from personal and work relationships to making a good first impression.

Question: How can I become aware of my emotions, and the feelings of others, and improve my communication with them?
Answer: Understanding emotions and identifying them is part of the skills that are part of emotional intelligence, though they do not involve everything. A person can be aware that they are angry or upset, yet take no action to control their outburst as a result. Emotional intelligence means they must recognize the potential for controlling their behavior as a result of their emotional state and respond appropriately. A matter won't be resolved if they become incensed and shout at people, who may avoid them completely. By thinking about how to respond in

an agitated state, which isn't always easy, an individual can thoroughly explain their dilemma and include more detail and information that may help give them better results. In turn, they are more likely to be heard and taken seriously, without any repercussions or fear of how they will react.

The capacity to not only recognize and understand your emotion but to respond to it appropriately must also be present as a part of EQ skills. This also applies when reading other people's emotions, as well. Reacting angrily to someone who hurls an insult will only result in further name-calling and escalation, whereas taking a more preventative approach or using a calmer tone to de-escalate can make a significant difference in the outcome of a situation.

Question: Isn't EQ all about empathy? As long as I have empathy, isn't that all I need to achieve emotional intelligence?

Answer: Essentially, EQ skills are based on empathy, which is one of the main attributes needed to improve your ability to understand and relate to others. In addition to possessing and demonstrating empathy, many other characteristics improve your EQ skills, including the ability to listen well and understand the true nature of someone's concerns and emotional state. Controlling your responses and communication with other people is another trait that goes beyond empathy and requires that you fully understand and identify with the other person. Focusing solely on empathy skews the full definition of emotional intelligence, and this is often a stereotype associated with this skill set. EQ goes beyond empathy to fully understand and recognize the importance of our behavior and actions based on emotion and how this impacts others. Self-management and awareness also play a key role in how we develop our emotional intelligence, which impacts our social skills as well.

Question: How can I influence someone else to change their behavior more positively?

Answer: There is no easy way to change a person's behavior unless they are open to doing so and recognize the need for positive change. Improving emotional intelligence gives us the skills to listen and understand the reasoning behind other people's actions and words, even if we can't change them. We can influence them by reacting to them in a positive, meaningful way that shows them we are listening and want to understand them more. This display of empathy often works to diffuse difficult situations, including explosive conflicts, where there doesn't seem to be a resolution available. Some people simply need space to vent or feel understood. Simply hearing them and giving them a non-judgmental platform to express their discontent can help them realize how to resolve the matter as well. We can offer advice, but more importantly, letting people communicate without conflict gives them a feeling of importance and consideration that may be missing in their life.

This can also change the direction of their behavior, even if just momentarily, so they can become part of the solution to their problem.

Question: Can a person build emotional intelligence when they have a habit of judging other people?

Answer: We are all guilty of passing judgment, even if it isn't too often. This can make it difficult to see past the conclusions we make when talking to someone. On the other hand, making a quick judgment about a person's mood or emotional state can help us to respond better, as we might have a stronger understanding of what they're going through and how to interact with them. Judging someone based on their appearance, social-economical status, and other criteria can be harmful, as it can often lead to false conclusions. When a person is judged, they usually know and will react accordingly. It may not be conveyed in how we speak to them, though our body language and gestures can give away what we feel. It is best to reserve judgment completely and focus on the person's needs and how we can help them. This approach will allow them to relax and respond more naturally and gives you a chance to do the same.

Question: How can I improve my relationship with someone who doesn't display any level of emotional intelligence?

Answer: There will always be people in our lives who cannot be met with reason. This includes people who do not have the capacity to understand nor control the behavior that stems from their emotions. This can be serious for long-term relationships and colleagues who may not express themselves adequately or without a clear message. The best you can do for people without a strong sense of EQ is continuing to listen to them and let them explain their point of view, even if you don't agree with them. There will always be difficult people who cannot be reasoned with, though most individuals respond favorably to patience and undivided attention, which is often what most people need to feel validated.

Question: What are some easy ways to show emotional intelligence?

Answer: Once you learn the basics, it's easy to follow for most people, though some important ways to exercise EQ skills, which include showing an interest in other people and engaging them socially. This can begin in a social setting, such as a party or event with coworkers or friends. You may notice body language and how gestures coincide with their overall message. By using observation as your main tool during interactions, you'll get to know how other people communicate with you both verbally and non-verbally. Emotions play a major role in how we behave and act in various situations. We must first acknowledge and understand our personal emotions before focusing on other people's feelings and behaviors. In many ways, we use EQ skills without thinking, by showing genuine concern and empathy for other people, acknowledging what someone else has to say, and validating their concerns, while actively showing that we are listening and taking everything seriously.

It is human nature to want to be understood and listened to. Strong listening skills can diffuse most arguments simply by hearing what the other person has to say. Often, conflict arises from a quick disagreement or interruption. By slowing down and taking the time to understand other people, we can avoid conflict in most cases, and instead, focus on building a positive relationship.

Question: If I work for an employer who does not value emotional intelligence as an assessment, am I likely to work with people who do not have this skill set?

Answer: Most employers include some aspect of EQ assessment or awareness, even if it is not included as a part of the recruitment process. You may hear your boss mention it to secure a new client or improve a relationship with a current customer. Making connections with colleagues and networking as a part of building your career is another way in which emotional intelligence plays a significant role, even if it is not directly addressed as such. Large corporations often include some components of their interview with EQ, though it is possible that some organizations skip this step completely, either because the job does not require much interaction with people or customers. On the other hand, there are many remote positions that include connecting with people, whether it's by virtual meetings or other ways of communicating online. Courtesy and etiquette in online communication is also a sign of strong EQ.

If an employer or company makes a point of not valuing EQ skills, or not taking them seriously, this can be a red flag that the organization may not be the best fit. As much as it is to our benefit to develop and improve emotional intelligence, it's just as vital to work and grow with people who adapt to the same way of communicating. An organization that doesn't take it seriously may experience a number of problems, including a lack of structure and respect among its staff, poor listening skills, and a lack of clear communication, favoritism, and other attributes that you would likely want to avoid, if possible. Some companies have been around for many years, and they do not lend their success to people skills, but products and brands that they sell and promote; you may find many of the staff are not as personable. If you've ever called a company to file a complaint or fix a problem with a product or service, pay close attention to the attitude and behavior of the representative. This will give you an idea of how well they are expected to conduct their business with you. Alternatively, representatives who engage in light conversation and give you the reassurance that your problem will be solved are likely trained and knowledgeable in EQ skills.

Question: If a person lacks empathy, how can they develop emotional intelligence?

Answer: There are some people who appear to lack the capacity for empathy, though for most individuals, caring for another person and showing genuine concern is a regular part of our lives, whether it's looking after aging parents, children, or customers at work. Even for people who may appear not to have feelings or emotional responses towards others, they often do, though they are careful and hesitant to display their feelings. In some cultures and practices, displays of emotion can be discouraged, which can make a person appear "cold" and unfeeling towards others, when they are grappling with their own emotions. There is a very small percentage of people without empathy, and even in these cases, progress can be made where a person is willing to observe and understand their emotions and others'.

Lacking empathy is a serious concern that impacts a small number of people, though most individuals will feel for another person and their situation, even if they don't share their thoughts. Showing emotion is not necessary to display empathy; you can merely identify with someone and show a degree of understanding about their plight and what they are going through. This will give the other person a sense of not feeling alone and that you are there for them. Consider some of the following examples of how you can use empathy to calm someone or give them a sense of hope or purpose:

- If a person is concerned about a lost pet, you may empathize with them by explaining how your pet did the same, and they were eventually found. Furthermore, you can relate to the concern and worry they have so that they don't feel alone in their situation.
- When someone relates a traumatic experience that you cannot personally relate to, you can show empathy by explaining how difficult you would find their situation to be if you were in their shoes, then give them credit for showing the courage to come forward and talk about it. Acknowledgment is a way to help someone feel empowered for sharing their story and giving it purpose and meaning.
- Finding common ground may not seem like empathy, but it can lead in this direction. For example, if a person has children, and you do as well, relating to them on what parents' experience can secure a bond with a strong level of trust. When there is an incident or situation, you may not always have the ability to relate entirely, though mentioning the difficulty of going through an event with a family and how hard it can be, shows empathy at the right time.

Question: How can my children learn emotional intelligence?

Answer: To a degree, some of the EQ skills children develop will occur naturally, though, like everyone, there is always room for improvement over time. Applying what you know to the relationship with your child can foster a deeper sense of trust and care that they can learn from as well. For most people, children, and adults alike, learning from others' experiences and observing is a powerful way to develop. Showing empathy to your children means they will learn how to practice this on their friends and others. General acts of kindness and displaying good listening skills when your children tell you about their day at school is vital. Often, we are too busy to listen for a longer time, due to many commitments in life, including work. Set aside time with your child to talk over various concerns and let them know that you can always be approached if they need you. Some of the best gifts we give our kids are in what they can learn from us, including the mistakes we make and how to connect better with each other. Emotional intelligence is a life-long process of learning and developing for everyone.

Question: Am I closer to getting hired if I display a good sense of emotional intelligence?

Answer: Yes, there is a good chance that your ability to connect with your potential employer with good social and emotional development skills will increase your employability. Showing your potential for emotional intelligence also provides you with a sense of confidence and an engaging personality that most people want to work for them. If you are self-employed, you'll want to exhibit the same traits to your clients as well. Making a good first impression is your best way to secure a good path towards a job. If you're uncertain of how to display your EQ at first and new to the process, make sure you listen and show your engagement during the interview with active gestures and non-verbal communication. If you need clarification or more information when a question is asked, don't hesitate to ask more about what is requested from you. A prospective employer will note this as active listening or a form of engagement, and also a sign of EQ. To further increase your chances of getting hired, always keep a few examples of emotional intelligence on the job-ready, just in case. This may include resolving customer relations matters or a conflict between coworkers. If you worked in a position with a high degree of stress, your ability to identify and handle stressors is also of value in the workplace. An employer will want to know how you can prevent serious issues, as well as resolving them using good social skills and empathy.

Question: If I'm already strong in EQ abilities, how can I know if there is room for improvement?

Answer: Everyone has room to improve and work on when it involves our social and professional connections with people. For some people, the professional connection on the job or in sales is excellent, while their personal relationships fail or are not as successful. Assess all your avenues for EQ skill-building, and determine which areas are best to improve. Even in situations where our emotional intelligence is strong, there may be some missed opportunities in getting a better assessment of the job or improving a friendship. If you ask someone for feedback about how you handle situations, this can offer a glimpse from another perspective, which is valuable and important as a learning tool. Often, we see in other people first what we fail to notice in ourselves. Once we recognize our own attributes through others, it can provide an experience that allows us to work on various aspects of our techniques.

Building strong emotional intelligence not only helps you to improve your relationships with other people, secure meaningful employment, and connect better with people; it is a great way to enhance your success in life and find more solutions to problems and issues in general. Developing good EQ skills can pave the road to a successful career while repairing and establishing better relationships with everyone in life in various circumstances. It's a form of self-improvement that also helps others.

CONCLUSION

Emotional intelligence is a powerful and useful way to develop interpersonal skills and understand the way we think and process feelings. It provides a deeper insight into how we communicate because of our feelings, and how other people do the same. Since its discovery, the study of EQ has grown into a network of research, assessment, and practical application in many aspects of everyday life. Today, most people know about emotional intelligence in a general sense and the importance of its role in employment and personal relationships. By learning about the advantages of EQ, you'll enjoy a much richer life and in your career. The many attributes of emotional intelligence, such as empathy, good listening skills, and focusing on the needs of others, are powerful ways to improve yourself in many ways.

In the professional realm, emotional intelligence is considered a priority in many sectors of employment. Most sectors of employment use EQ assessments as an important part of the recruitment process, which makes it a vital set of skills to develop for both professional and personal reasons. It's a set of skills that must be continuously improved upon and practiced to maintain a sharp and effective level. Anyone can possess a strong foundation of emotional intelligence, though it is best to continuously improve upon for best results in the job marketplace. A skilled human resources consultant will likely be able to notice a strong sense or lack of EQ abilities within a short time frame. For people who generally lack emotional intelligence, developing a strong sense of self-awareness is one of the most important aspects of establishing EQ skills. While most people develop characteristics in childhood, emotional intelligence continues to improve or change throughout adulthood as well.

Emotional intelligence is one of the most human ways to develop adequate skills for life. You'll have access to better jobs, stronger connections with people, and an improved understanding of how people express their emotions. Understanding can make a major difference in many scenarios, as one of the most common reasons for arguments and conflict is simply a lack of knowing more about others, their fears, and concerns. Which can make a significant impact on how we interact with one another. In many ways, studying the effects of EQ and working towards improving our skills in this area can open many new opportunities for personal and professional growth and improvement for life.

DESCRIPTION

What is emotional intelligence, and how does it play a role in our lives? For many employers and professionals, the evaluation of an individual's EQ level is a vital step in assessing their fitness for the job, whether it's at the application or interview stage of the recruitment process. As EQ quickly rose to popularity in the early 1990s, many people questioned the validity of its purpose and how effective it is in everyday life. Today, most employers consider emotional intelligence as one of the critical components in assessing the fitness of a candidate or potential employee. In this book, you will learn the basics characteristics of emotional intelligence, and how developing these skills can vastly improve your chances of landing your next job, or improving relationships within your family, friendship and among colleagues, and:

- How to identify key signs of emotional intelligence in other people
- The main characteristics of EQ and how they can benefit you in your personal and professional relationships
- The history and research behind emotional intelligence and how it all began
- You are developing the fundamentals of EQ and how to apply it on the job, at home, and in your immediate community.
- Useful tools and techniques for learning and implementing self-improvement and self-awareness
- The pros and cons of measuring emotional intelligence and why most employers regard it as vital
- How improving your EQ level can help improve your employability

For people already knowledgeable about emotional intelligence, there are many myths and misperceptions about the skill set and what it means to them. EQ can be a natural way for some people, and more challenging for others to learn and adapt to. With practice, anyone can know and implement attributes associated with empathy, listening skills, and other valuable tools that build EQ:

- Making your best first impression by increasing your emotional intelligence
- Recognizing areas for improvement
- How to apply EQ in everyday situations and how to foster deeper relationships for personal and professional benefits at school, work, and home.
- It is debunking the myths about EQ and why it is often misunderstood.
- Empathy's Role in interpersonal relationships and developing strong social skills and networking

Emotional intelligence plays a role in how we succeed in life and our relationships with other people, often without our knowledge that we are using it. If you are a good listener or actively engage with someone to highlight their concerns, you are on the right path already! Empathy is a powerful way to show someone that you are there to listen without judgment. In learning about EQ skills, you will discover many fascinating and essential characteristics about the people you work and associate with while sharpening your abilities to become a better person for the job and secure a stronger friendship or connection with someone. As we continue to evolve and grow, emotional intelligence will continuously play a vital role in how we develop and connect with everyone. Starting within, learning about the connection between feelings and how subsequent reaction and behavior is the best place to begin to create your own EQ tool kit.

COGNITIVE BEHAVIORAL THERAPY

Retrain Your Brain, Improve Self-Esteem and Self-Discipline, Learn Emotional Intelligence and Change Your Life

Nicole Gladwell

© Copyright 2020 by Nicole Gladwell. All right reserved.

The work contained herein has been produced with the intent to provide relevant knowledge and information on the topic on the topic described in the title for entertainment purposes only. While the author has gone to every extent to furnish up to date and true information, no claims can be made as to its accuracy or validity as the author has made no claims to be an expert on this topic. Notwithstanding, the reader is asked to do their own research and consult any subject matter experts they deem necessary to ensure the quality and accuracy of the material presented herein.

This statement is legally binding as deemed by the Committee of Publishers Association and the American Bar Association for the territory of the United States. Other jurisdictions may apply their own legal statutes. Any reproduction, transmission, or copying of this material contained in this work without the express written consent of the copyright holder shall be deemed as a copyright violation as per the current legislation in force on the date of publishing and the subsequent time thereafter. All additional works derived from this material may be claimed by the holder of this copyright.

The data, depictions, events, descriptions, and all other information forthwith are considered to be true, fair, and accurate unless the work is expressly described as a work of fiction. Regardless of the nature of this work, the Publisher is exempt from any responsibility of actions taken by the reader in conjunction with this work. The Publisher acknowledges that the reader acts of their own accord and releases the author and Publisher of any responsibility for the observance of tips, advice, counsel, strategies, and techniques that may be offered in this volume.

INTRODUCTION

Cognitive Behavioral Therapy has been an increasingly hot topic in psychology in the past few years. More and more therapists and psychiatrists adapt to this type of speaking therapy due to its proven effectiveness in treating common mental disorders like anxiety and depression. In this book, you will learn about CBT in great depth, including the following topics in particular;

What You Will Learn in This Book
This book will explore the theories and functions of Cognitive Behavioral Therapy and how it works to treat disorders like Anxiety and Depression. We will start this book by learning more about how CBT works when used and how it compares to other therapy types. We will then learn about what anxiety is, its symptoms, and different styles. We will then learn about depression, the science behind it, the different types, and its symptoms. By this point in the book, you should have a strong understanding of how anxiety and depression work and how CBT can effectively treat symptoms. Towards this book's center, we will be looking at the benefits and drawbacks of choosing CBT as your treatment method. This chapter is essential in determining if CBT is the right treatment method for the disorder you are looking to treat. After that, we will focus on using CBT to specifically manage a person's anxiety/depression and use other methods to manage these disorders. We will take a look into mindfulness, meditation, lifestyle changes, and practicing gratitude.

Who This Book Is for
Are you someone that feels like their mental disorders always burden them? Do you feel like something is holding you back from reaching your full potential? Are you feeling stuck and are struggling to get out of this slump? If you identify with this, this book can help you learn Cognitive Behavioral Therapy to treat your disorders. Still, it will also equip you with the right knowledge to understand what is happening and why. It is crucial to learn as much as you can regarding your mental health, and from there, apply the CBT methods you will learn to treat your situation correctly.

Overall, I wrote this book to teach you how to use CBT and educate you on all topics related to understanding why CBT uses its strategy. Understanding that, people are more likely to stay committed to the process than give up if they don't see results right away. Without further ado, let's dive into this book.

CHAPTER 1
What Is Cognitive Behavioral Therapy?

Cognitive Behavioral Therapy has been an increasingly hot topic in psychology in the past few years. More and more therapists and psychiatrists adapt to this type of speaking therapy due to its proven effectiveness in treating common mental disorders like anxiety and depression. Although we hear about this term a lot, what exactly is it? This chapter will look at what Cognitive Behavioral Therapy is and when you can use it.

What Is Cognitive Behavioral Therapy (CBT)?

So, what exactly is it? The foundation of Cognitive Behavioral Therapy is the theory that a person's thoughts (cognition), emotion, and behavior are all constantly interacting with one another; therefore, if one of these three components are affected, the rest will be affected as well. CBT is an umbrella term for many different therapies that share standard details.

The three components that Cognitive Behavioral Therapy (CBT) focuses on are the following;

CognitionResponsible for how we think and what we think.

- Emotion

Based on how we feel.

- Behavior

Based on how we act.

These three components all support the theory that if a person merely changes their thoughts or the way they think, it will impact their feelings, ultimately determining their behavior.

In simple terms, this means that people who may be having negative or unrealistic thoughts that cause them distress could result in behavioral problems. When a person is suffering from psychological pain, they perceive certain situations that can become contorted, causing negative behaviors.

How Does CBT Work?

Cognitive Behavioral Therapy works by emphasizing the relationship between our thoughts, feelings, and behaviors. When you begin to change any of these components, you start to initiate change in the others. CBT aims to help lower the amount you worry and increase the overall quality of your life.

Here are the eight basic principles of how Cognitive Behavioral Therapy works:

1. CBT will help provide a new perspective of understanding your problems.

Often, when an individual has been living with a problem for a long time in their life, they may have developed unique ways of understanding it and dealing with it. Usually, this just maintains the problem or makes it worse. CBT is useful in helping you look at your situation from a new perspective, and this will help you learn other ways of understanding your problem and learning a new way of dealing with it.

2. CBT will help you generate new skills to work out your problem. You probably know that understanding a problem is one matter, and dealing with it is entirely another can of worms. To help start changing your situation, you will need to develop new skills to transform your thoughts, behaviors, and emotions that affect your anxiety and mental health. For instance, CBT will help you achieve new ideas about your problem and begin to use and test them in your daily life. Therefore, you will be more capable of making up your mind regarding the root issue causing these negative symptoms.

3. CBT relies on teamwork and collaboration between the client and therapist (or program).

CBT will require you to be actively involved in the entire process, and your thoughts and ideas are extremely valuable right from the beginning of the therapy. You are the expert when it comes to your thoughts and problems. The therapist is the expert when it comes to acknowledging the emotional issues. By working as a team, you will identify your problems and have your therapist better address them. Historically, the more the therapy advances, the more the client finds techniques to deal with the symptoms.

4. The goal of CBT is to help the client become their therapist.

Therapy is expensive; we all know that. One of CBT's goals is not to have you become overly dependent on your therapist because it is not feasible to have therapy forever. When treatment comes to an end, and you do not become your therapist, you will be at high risk for a relapse. However, if you can become your therapist, you will be in a good spot to face the hurdles that life throws at you. Also, scientists proved that having confidence in your ability to face hardship is one of the best predictors of maintaining the valuable information you got from therapy. By playing an active role during your sessions, you will gain the confidence needed to face your problems when the sessions are over.

5. CBT is brief and time-limited.

As a rule of thumb, CBT therapy sessions typically last from 10 to 20 sessions. Statistically, when therapy goes on for many months, there is a higher risk of the client becoming dependent on the therapist. Once you have gained a new perspective and understanding of your problem and have equipped yourself with the right skills, you can solve future problems. It is crucial in CBT for you to try out your new skills in the real world. By actually dealing with your own problem hands-on without the security of recurring therapy sessions, you will be able to build confidence in your ability to become your therapist.

6. CBT is direction based and structured.

CBT typically relies on a fundamental strategy called 'guided recovery.' By setting up some experiments with your therapist, you will be able to experiment with new ideas to see if they reflect your reality accurately. In other words, your therapist is your guide while you are making discoveries in CBT. The therapist will not tell you whether you are right or wrong, but instead, they will help develop ideas and experiments to test these ideas.

7. CBT is based on the present, "here and now."

Although we know that our childhood and developmental history play a significant role in who we are today, one of CBT's principles is looking at the relationship between what caused the problem and what maintains the problem presently. In many cases, the reasons that maintain a problem are different from those that initially caused it. For example, if you fall off while riding a horse, you may become afraid of horses. Your fear will continue to be maintained if you begin avoiding all horses and refusing to ride one again. In this example, the fall caused anxiety, but you continue to maintain it by avoiding fear. Unfortunately, you cannot change the fact that you had fallen off the horse, but you can change your behaviors when it comes to avoidance. CBT primarily focuses on the factors that are maintaining the problem because these factors are susceptible to change.

8. Worksheet exercises are significant elements of CBT therapy.

Unfortunately, reading about CBT or going to one therapy session a week is not enough to change our ingrained patterns of thinking and behaving. During CBT, the client is always encouraged to apply their new skills into their daily lives. Although most people find CBT therapy sessions very intriguing, it does not lead to change in reality if you do not exercise the skills you have learned.

These eight principles will be your guiding light throughout your Cognitive Behavioral Therapy. By learning, understanding, and applying these eight principles, you will be in an excellent position to invest your time and energy into becoming your therapist and start reaching your goals. Based on research, individuals who are highly motivated to try exercises outside of sessions tend to find more value in therapy than those who don't. Keep in mind that other external factors still affect your success, but your motivation is one of the most significant factors. By following CBT using the principles above, you should be able to remain highly motivated throughout CBT.

The History of CBT

Albert Ellis and Aaron T. Beck developed the earliest forms of cognitive-behavioral therapy in the mid-90s. At the time, it was called Rational Emotive Behavior Therapy (REBT). REBT is a type of cognitive therapy that focuses on fixing emotional and behavioral problems. The main goal of REBT is to shift irrational beliefs to rational ones. Rational Emotive Behavior Therapy encourages an individual to figure out their irrational personal beliefs and then influence them to challenge those beliefs by testing them in reality.

Albert Ellis proposed that every single person carries a unique set of assumptions regarding ourselves and our world. He suggested that we use that set of beliefs to serve and guide us through life and has a significant influence on our reactions to different situations that we experience. However, some people's set of assumptions are irrational, leading to them acting and reacting in inappropriate ways and can even inhibit your success. This term is called 'basic irrational assumptions.'

An example of an irrational assumption will be if an individual assumes they are a failure because everyone they know doesn't express love for them. This assumption leads them to be seeking out approval and feeling rejected constantly. Since this individual sees all actions and interactions from the lens of this assumption, they will feel dissatisfied if they did not receive enough compliments. According to Albert Ellis, these are other popular and common irrational assumptions:

- The idea that you should be competent at everything you do
- The idea that when things are not the way you want them to be it is catastrophic
- The idea that you cannot control your happiness
- The idea that you need to be dependent on somebody stronger than you
- The idea that your history heavily influences your present life
- The idea that it will be a disaster if you don't find the perfect solution to human problems

Aaron Beck has a similar therapy system to Albert Ellis's, but his version is more common for treating depression than anxiety. Therapists typically use this therapy system to help the client notice the negative thoughts and logic errors that lead them to be depressed. They also use this system to challenge an individual's dysfunctional thoughts, try to interpret situations differently, and apply a different perspective of thinking into their everyday lives.

Typically, if a person has many negative automatic thoughts, it is likely that they would become depressed. These thoughts will continue even though there is conflicting evidence. Aaron Beck identified three mechanisms in the mid-90s that he thought caused depression:

- The cognitive triad (automatic negative thinking)
- Negative self-schemas
- Errors in logic (inaccurate information processing)

Aaron Beck posited that "the cognitive triad" includes three harmful thinking types that individuals suffer from depression showcase. It consisted of negative thoughts about yourself, the world, and the future.

These types of thoughts tend to appear automatically in depressed people and are quite spontaneous. As these three types of thoughts begin to interact, they interfere with our brain's normal cognitive functions and lead to perception impairment, memory impairment, and difficulty with problem-solving. The person will likely become obsessed with these negative thoughts.

Aaron Beck identified numerous illogical thinking processes in his study of cognitive distortions. He concluded that these irrational thought patterns are self-deprecating and cause many anxieties and depression symptoms. Here are a few of his irrational thinking processes:

- Arbitrary interference: This thinking process involves concluding with insufficient and irrelevant evidence. For instance, thinking and feeling worthless because of the theme park you were going to have closed due to weather.
- Selective Abstraction: This thinking process involves focusing on one aspect of a circumstance and ignoring all other elements. For example, you feel responsible for your team losing a volleyball match even though you are just one team member.
- Magnification: The thinking process involves the exaggeration of importance during a negative situation. For example, if you accidentally scratched your car, you see yourself as a terrible driver.
- Minimization: This thinking process involves underplaying the importance of an event. For instance, you get praised by your boss for your excellent work, but you see this is a trivial matter.
- Overgeneralization: This thinking process involves drawing negative conclusions due to one single event. For example, you usually get straight As in university, but you failed one exam, and therefore, you think you are stupid.
- Personalization: This thinking process involves associating the negative feelings of other people with yourself. For example, your boss looked angry when she entered the office today; therefore, she must be angry with you.

Aaron Beck and Albert Ellis have developed many theories and structured behaviors that led to the modern-day development of Cognitive Behavioral Therapy. Due to their research in the mid-90s, studies have concluded that 80% of adults benefit from Cognitive Behavioral Therapy. This result is a massive success in therapy, as many people prefer talking therapy over medical treatment to help mental disorders like anxiety and depression.

CBT Today

In today's society, Cognitive Behavioral Therapy is used to treat mental disorders, primarily anxiety and depression. We will look at these treatments in more detail in further chapters of this book.

Due to its long history and development, CBT is a practical and time-saving form of psychotherapy. CBT focuses on your here-and-now problems that come up in daily life. It helps people make sense of their surroundings and events that happen around them. CBT is very structured, time-saving, and problem-focused. These advantages are why CBT is one of the most popular techniques for dealing with mental disorders in our fast-paced modern lives.

In the present day, CBT works by helping clients recognize, question, and change the thoughts that relate to the emotional and behavioral reactions that cause them difficulty. Using CBT to monitor and record thoughts during undesirable situations, people begin to learn that the way they think contributes to their emotional problems. Modern-day Cognitive Behavioral Therapy helps reduce emotional problems by teaching individuals to:

- Identify any distortions in their thinking process
- See their thoughts as ideas rather than facts
- Take a step back from their thoughts to look at situations from another perspective

The new CBT model used in the present day focuses on the relationship between thoughts and behaviors. Both can influence each other. There are three levels and types of thoughts:

- Conscious thoughts: These are rational thoughts that people think with complete awareness
- Automatic thoughts: These are the thoughts that move very quickly; you are likely not to be fully aware of their movement. For this reason, it is difficult to check them for accuracy. A person suffering from mental health problems may have thoughts that are entirely not logical.
- Schemas: These are the core beliefs and personal values when it comes to processing information. Our childhood and other life experiences shape our Schemas.

The modern-day CBT is slightly different from the previous type, which was mainly REBT. The CBT we use now is used to treat a plethora of mental disorders, whereas we used REBT in the past, mostly to treat depression and anxiety. Moreover, depression and anxiety were not as prevalent in the mid-90s compared to its presence now. In the later chapters, we will discuss why mental orders like depression and anxiety are more common in today's society.

Who Uses CBT?

Many people use Cognitive Behavioral Therapy, whether it is to help others or solve their problems. The most general answer to who uses CBT would be a therapist and somebody with a mental disorder. However, CBT professionals use it within the psychology space, alcohol addiction, substance abuse, eating disorders, phobias, and anger management. CBT is a flexible tool that many types of people can use to treat the problem at hand.

CBT can benefit you even if you are not facing a severe problem like mentioned above. Many people who used to go to therapy continue to use CBT to maintain a healthy mindset. CBT has also proved useful for events like interventions. However, the people that typically use and gain the most from CBT are the people who are willing to spend the time and energy analyzing their thoughts and feelings. Since self-analysis generally is difficult, many people may give up after realizing how uncomfortable it could be. However, CBT is very well-suited for the people looking for short term treatment that does not require medication. This strategy is very suitable for people who don't want to take drugs to manage disorders like depression and anxiety.

CHAPTER 2
When Is Cognitive Behavioral Therapy Used?

When Is CBT Used?

Now that you have learned how CBT works in the first chapter of this book, we will look at why CBT is a method of choice for professionals worldwide.

The main answer to this question is that professionals use CBT to pursue therapy to help their clients with their problems. These problems are often disorders such as depression, anxiety, or more serious ones like OCD and PTSD.

The most common uses for CBT are depression and generalized anxiety disorder to dive a little more in-depth. However, CBT is also used and is very useful for other conditions such as:

- Body Dysmorphic Disorder
- Eating Disorders
- Chronic Low Back Pain
- Personality Disorders
- Psychosis
- Schizophrenia
- Substance Used Disorders

Since CBT focuses on the relationship between thoughts, emotions, and behavior, those who suffer from disorders that stem from mental health may find it helpful to try CBT. Most modern-day therapists opt for CBT as the best technique to handle the client's problems as it covers numerous disorders, and the client can learn it and continue to use it without the therapist's help.

On a more straightforward note, professionalism as a method of general therapy. Professionals could choose this when they attend therapy sessions to remain in touch with their thoughts and feelings. Although this person may not be suffering from any particular disorder, CBT is a helpful tool for someone who wants to organize their thoughts.

CBT and Other Methods of Therapy

Cognitive Behavioral Therapy and other types of behavioral therapies share a lot in common and have many significant differences. The typical behavioral therapies that you may see on TV and movies seem to involve a lot of dream interpretation or complex discussion of childhood experiences. This type of therapy is very outdated compared to CBT. Not many therapists in modern-day use this type of treatment. CBT is different from other therapies by focusing mainly on how a person's thoughts, emotions, and behaviors are connected.

Examples of Other Types of Therapy
In this section, we will look at other types of therapy and how they compare to CBT. Although CBT is an effective treatment for anxiety and depression, there are alternate methods to help its effectiveness if we practice them simultaneously. Techniques such as mindfulness and meditation, improving your physical health, preventing bad habits like procrastination, and practicing gratitude go a long way in managing anxiety and depression. Let's take a look at these other methods.

- Psychodynamic or Psychoanalytic Psychotherapy

In psychodynamic (or psychoanalytic psychotherapy), the therapist helps the person open up, speak about their thoughts, and express their feelings. After listening to you open up, the therapist will tell you what they observe, such as patterns or problems in your life or your ways of thinking.

Psychodynamic therapy is similar to psychoanalytic therapy in that it is an in-depth form of talk-therapy based on principles and theories of psychoanalysis. However, psychodynamic therapy is not as focused on the relationship between the client and therapist but focuses on the client's relationship with their external world. Usually, psychodynamic therapy does not last as long as psychoanalytic therapy when it comes to the number of sessions and the frequency of those sessions; however, this differs by case.

Psychodynamic therapy is commonly used to treat depression or anxiety and other severe psychological disorders. It focuses primarily on the people who may have lost meaning in their lives and struggle to maintain and form personal relationships. Studies have found that people who suffer from eating disorders, addiction, and social anxiety disorders benefit from psychodynamic therapy. During psychodynamic therapy, the client is encouraged to speak about anything that comes to mind, including dreams, desires, fantasies, current issues, and the therapist's help. This therapy aims to reduce their depression or anxiety systems and achieve other benefits such as better use of their abilities and talents, increasing self-esteem, and an improved ability to develop and maintain better relationships. The client may continue to experience the benefits even after this therapy has ended. Some patients may find that short-term therapy (less than one year) is sufficient; some other patients may require long-term therapy to gain lasting effects.

Psychodynamic therapy's theories and techniques distinguish it from other forms of therapy. Psychodynamic therapy focuses on acknowledging, recognizing, expressing, understanding, and overcoming contradictory and negative feelings and repressed emotions to improve a person's interpersonal relationships and experiences. Psychodynamic therapy helps the client understand how their previous repressed emotions affect their current behavior, relationships, and decision-making. This type of therapy also aims to help the client who may be aware of their social difficulties but doesn't have the tools or skills to overcome this problem by themselves. During this therapy, the clients will learn to analyze and resolve their current issues and then change their behavior in their existing relationships by using in-depth exploration and analysis of their past experiences and emotions.

- Cognitive Analytical Therapy (CAT)

Cognitive analytical therapy combines CBT and psychodynamic psychotherapy to develop a new hybrid form of therapy. It focuses on your behavior and how this may be causing problems in your life. Then, the therapist presents you with solutions.

- Interpersonal Psychotherapy (IPT)

Interpersonal psychotherapy focuses on a person's relationships and how these could lead to mental illness. This type of therapy includes looking at relationship breakdown, disputing, or other events involving relationships that could cause a person's internal struggles. Then, the therapist will help you to find strategies for dealing with this.

Interpersonal psychotherapy (IPT) is evidence-based, focused, and time-limited approach to treat mental disorders like depression and anxiety. The primary goal of IPT is to improve the quality of a person's social functioning and interpersonal relationships to reduce their distress in those situations. There are four main areas with which IPT helps the client. Firstly, it focuses on addressing interpersonal deficits, such as involvement in unfulfilling relationships and social isolation. Secondly, IPT helps clients manage their unresolved grief, especially if the reason for their distress is related to the loss of a close person in their lives either in the past or recently. Thirdly, IPT can also help with challenging life changes such as moving to another city, divorce, or retirement. Lastly, IPT also helps people dealing with conflict-related relationships such as with co-workers, family members, close friends, or partners.

Scientists initially developed IPT to treat major depressive disorders (MDD). It is also effectively used to treat perinatal depression, eating disorders, drug, and alcohol abuse, dysthymia, and other mood disorders such as bipolar disorder (BPD). IPT is different from traditional therapy types by focusing on the present rather than past relationships or upbringing. This practice is different from CBT because it speaks to maladaptive thoughts and behaviors and how they affect relationships.

The goal of IPT is to change a person's relationship patterns and not their depressive symptoms and target relationship struggles that exacerbate the symptoms. IPT is less structured than CBT as it focuses on the areas that the client has specified without concentrating on their personality traits.

Treatment using IPT usually is in individual therapy sessions and group work that is completed anywhere from 12 weeks to 16 weeks. Its methodology is structured daily and includes assessments throughout the treatment, interviews with the therapist, and homework exercises. The first stage of IPT requires the therapist to assess the client's social history and depressive symptoms within the first three sessions. They examine the client's social history in-depth, noting any changes in the patterns of their relationships. After that, the therapist and client will work as a team to implement the treatment strategies chosen specifically to areas with the most problems. As treatment develops, they may change their targeted problem area. Group sessions are similar to the individual ones because they are semi-structured, focused on interpersonal dynamics, and are time-limited. Group therapies provide clients a safe and supportive environment to practice their interpersonal skills. Pre, mid, and post-treatment sessions also occur in a group therapy format to review the client's individual progress, goals, and strategies.

IPT was developed over 20 years ago and originally intended to be a time-structured treatment for people who had severe depression or anxiety. In recent years, it gained a lot of popularity. IPT practitioners believe that changing a person's social environment is an essential factor in treating depression or anxiety and preventing it. In the beginning, therapists used IPT exclusively for adults, but it has been modified in recent years, so adolescents and older people can benefit.

- Humanistic Therapy

Humanistic therapy is focused on positive psychology and helping a person increase their self-awareness and image of themselves.

- Family and Couple or Systemic Therapies

Family or couples therapy is a kind of group therapy that involves several people who are in close relationships who wish to work through problems together with a therapist's help.

- Mindfulness and Meditation

The most commonly practiced meditation is mindfulness meditation. Mindfulness meditation is a type of mental training practice that focuses your mind on your thoughts and sensations in the present moment. These include; your current emotions, physical feelings, and passing thoughts. Mindfulness meditation usually involves breathing practice, mental imagery, awareness of your mind and body, and muscle and body relaxation. It is typically more accessible for beginners to follow a guided meditation directing them throughout the whole process. It is extremely easy to drift away or fall asleep while in meditation if nobody is guiding you. Once you become more skilled in mindfulness meditation, you can do it without a vocal guide, but this requires strong mental capabilities.

- Medical Treatment

When it comes to anti-depressants, it is the most advertised treatment for depression and anxiety, but it doesn't necessarily mean that it is the most effective. Depression is about chemical imbalances in the brain, but it does not mean that it is only that. Medication can often help relieve moderate to severe depression symptoms, but it does not solve the underlying problem and is not a long-term solution. Like we learned previously, antidepressants come with side effects, and if a person does not wean off properly, they can suffer from withdrawal.

Antidepressants and Anti-anxiety medications are a range of drugs that treat depression, anxiety, and a variety of other mental disorders. They are the most commonly prescribed medications these days. Antidepressants include SSRIs (serotonin reuptake inhibitors), SNRIs (serotonin-norepinephrine reuptake inhibitors), TCAs (tricyclic antidepressants), atypical antidepressants, and MAOIs (monoamine oxidase inhibitors).

Antidepressants and Anti-anxiety medications work by adjusting the brain's neurotransmitters to help correct the balance of chemicals. When a person is in the trenches of torment, depression's pain, and anguish, merely taking a pill can seem like a simple and convenient relief method. However, it is essential to keep in mind that brain chemicals' imbalance isn't the only cause of depression. Instead, it is a combination of that and other psychological, biological, and social factors that include coping skills, relationships, and lifestyle, all of which medication would not address. However, it does not mean the antidepressants are not sufficient. When a person's depression is on a severe level, antidepressants can be lifesaving or very helpful. Although medication can help people relieve some of their symptoms, antidepressants do not cure depression and are not a recommended long-term solution. However, as more time goes by, people who originally had found antidepressants to be useful can fall back into depression. This effect can happen to the people who stop taking the medication. Antidepressants also come with undesirable side effects, so people need to consider the pros and cons of taking depression medication if you are considering it.

Comparisons Between CBT and Other Therapies
Both CBT and other behavioral therapies have common approaches, such as:
- The therapist and client work as a team to understand that the client is the expert on their thoughts while the therapist has theoretical and technical expertise.
- Treatments are often short term (usually lasting between 6 - 20 sessions). The client actively participates in the treatment inside and outside of the sessions. Homework and worksheets are often mandatory.
- The therapist aims to help the client realize that they are strong and capable of choosing to have positive thoughts and behaviors.

- Treatment is aimed to resolve present-day problems and is goal-oriented. The therapy involves achieving goals by working step by step.
- The client and therapist choose their goals for therapy together and track their progress throughout the treatment.

The foundation of CBT is the theory that thoughts influence feelings and that a person's emotional response to a problem comes from how they interpreted the situation. Here's an example to help you further understand: Imagine feeling your heart's sensations beating irregularly fast and feeling shortness of breath. If these symptoms occurred while you were sitting quietly at home, you would likely assume that it is a medical condition like a heart attack, which will cause anxiety and worry. However, if these symptoms occurred while you were running outside, you would likely not attribute it to a medical condition, and therefore it will not lead to anxiety and worry. Do you see here that different interpretations of the same sensations (e.g., heart racing and shortness of breath) can lead to different emotions entirely?

CBT suggests that many of the emotions that we are feeling are entirely due to the thoughts that we are thinking. In other words, our feelings come from how we perceive and interpret our environment or a situation. Sometimes these ideas and thoughts become distorted or biased. For example, an individual may interpret an ambiguous text message as personal rejection when they may not have any evidence to support that. Other individuals may begin to set unrealistic expectations for themselves regarding being accepted by others. These thoughts contribute to illogical, biased, or distorted thinking processes, which then affect our emotions. In CBT, clients will learn to distinguish the difference between an actual thought and feeling. They will learn to be aware of how thoughts can influence their emotions and how it is sometimes unhelpful. They will also critically evaluate whether their automatic thoughts are accurate and have evidence, or if they are simply just biased. At the end of their therapy, they should have developed the skills to notice these negative thoughts, interrupt them, and correct the thoughts properly.

Now, let's talk about how other behavioral therapies are different. Most of them focus on how specific thoughts and behaviors are accidentally "rewarded" within an individual's environment. These rewards contribute to these thoughts and behaviors increasing. Behavior therapies assist with a wide selection of psychological symptoms in a wide range of ages. Here are a couple of examples to further explain it:
- Example #1:

Imagine a teenager who continually asks for permission to use the family car to hang out with friends. After the parents asking repeatedly and receiving numerous denials, the teenager becomes angry and disobedient towards the parents. Afterward, the parents conclude that they do not want to take the hassle from their teen anymore and allow their teen to borrow the car. By giving permission, the teenager has received a "reward" for throwing a tantrum. Behavior therapists say that by permitting the teenager, the teenager has learned that bad behavior is a strategy that works if they are going after permission. Moreover, behavior therapy aims to understand the relationships between behaviors, rewards, and learning and change negative patterns. In conclusion, the parents and children in this example can unlearn these unhealthy behaviors and reinforce good behavior instead.

- Example #2:

Imagine being afraid to ride in vehicles. To avoid being scared and anxious, you may eventually begin to avoid all vehicles and walk or ride a bicycle instead. The extra energy and time required for your transportation may cause you to be always late for events or work. Despite these consequences, however, your fear of riding in a car has been rewarded with an absence of fear and anxiety. Behavioral treatments would consist of riding in a car under a supervised environment and reward you when you are successful. These rewards come after each success, and it aims to help you unlearn these negative associations. Although behavioral therapies are different based on the disorder they are treating, a common thread is that behavioral therapists help their clients try new or feared behaviors and disallows them from letting negative rewards dictate their behavior.

A Blended Approach

We talked about the three main types of psychotherapy which is CBT, IPT, and psychodynamic therapy. There is another common approach- the blended approach. A blended approach could include either a blend of a few different psychotherapies or one kind of psychotherapy, including integrated talking therapies and digital content. For instance, while a person is going through CBT, they may be given homework through educational modules or apps to monitor their sleep or mood. This information usually helps the therapist have reflective conversations with the client.

Blended approaches of psychotherapy haven't fully developed or enmeshed into mental health services at the grand scale. Researchers are still studying the best methods to integrate digital content with the traditional face to face therapy, as well as how they can collect evidence on the effectiveness of it all. In a general sense, identifying barriers and facilitators for these digital methods has been a distinguishing line of work over recent years as this method is growing in popularity. For instance, some people may not have the means to pay for a therapist, so they can opt for CBT programs online or through a self-help book to self-direct their therapy and learning. This field is an excellent area of opportunity for researchers to study.

The Pros and Cons of CBT

In this section, we will look at CBT's pros and cons to give you an idea of the real-world benefits that it can provide you with and some of the challenges that come with it.

The Benefits of CBT

1. Studies have found research that shows that cognitive-behavioral therapy is as effective as medication in treating anxiety disorders and other mental health disorders.
2. CBT is time-sensitive - Completed in a short amount of time compared with other types of behavioral therapies.
3. CBT is highly structured, which means that therapists can conduct it in different formats. These formats include self-help books, groups, and computer programs.
4. During CBT, you learn valuable and practical skills that you can incorporate into your daily life. These skills can help you cope with current stresses and future difficulties as well.

The Drawbacks of CBT

1. To fully benefit from CBT, you need to commit to the process. A therapist can help and advise, but they cannot help solve your problems without your cooperation.
2. CBT's structured nature may not be suitable for people suffering from learning disabilities or more complex mental health problems.
3. Some people argue that CBT only helps with current problems and specific issues; it fails to address the possibility of underlying mental health issues. For example, an unhappy childhood.
4. CBT often focuses on the individual's ability to change their thoughts, feelings, and behaviors but does not address a more comprehensive set of problems regarding systems or families. These problems typically have a significant impact on somebody's health and wellbeing.

Overall, CBT is very useful in helping people manage their problems, such as depressive or anxious thoughts, to make it less likely to negatively impact a person's life. However, there is always a risk that the feelings you associate with your problems will return, but if you understand and know how to use your CBT skills, it should be easy for you to control them. If you practice CBT with a therapist or through a program, it is essential to practice your learned skills even when the sessions are over.

The Science Behind CBT

A constant theme in the later chapters of this book is that CBT is a complicated process, and it requires a lot of effort and commitment for the client to achieve the benefits. For those who are learning about cognitive behavioral therapy for the first time, homework and practice may be challenging and grueling at first. When people start CBT with their therapist, they will tell the client that they need to start very small with their initial changes. Like any habit that we develop, it takes a lot of time and self-discipline to get to the point where you don't have to think about it anymore.

In many cases, the first step and change you have to make using CBT is simply being aware of your thoughts. You don't necessarily have to try to change them yet, but you will begin to notice some unhealthy thinking styles you may have by starting to be aware of them.

The theory behind CBT is that an individual's thoughts, emotions, and behaviors are all connected. Creating small changes in your life will help you start to change your thoughts, which will influence a change in your emotions and behaviors. Here are a couple of tips on small changes you can make in your daily life:

- Balance your thoughts.

If you're suffering from a mental health disorder, you tend to have distressing and flawed thoughts, influencing your behavior. For example, if you get anxious in social situations, you tend to avoid them actively. Your mind automatically tells you that you would panic and do something embarrassing if you get yourself in a social situation. This belief would then reinforce your thoughts and avoidance of social situations. By balancing your thoughts, you begin to analyze your thought processes and see the error of your ways. By merely just paying attention to these automatic thoughts that lead to your beliefs, you may slowly be able to change your thought process, which would ultimately adjust your beliefs.

- Change your point of view.

Once you have established the ability to notice your thoughts simply, you can begin changing your perspective. By recognizing your cognitive distortions or unhelpful thinking styles, you can start to use a technique called cognitive restructuring to help transform your undesirable thoughts simply. In return, your behavior will change, as well. The next time you start to feel the emotions of anxiety, try asking yourself: "What thoughts am I having right now that are causing these emotions to arise?" By identifying the thoughts that are causing you distress, you can then restructure those thoughts to be helpful instead of problematic. As you notice the specific thoughts or memories causing you distress, you can write them down in a list. Writing them down will help you remember some recurring thoughts that then lead to negative emotions and behavior. Ultimately, this will help you understand how your thoughts are connected to your feelings and determine your trigger stimulus.

- Have patience with yourself.

As has been emphasized throughout this book, CBT takes time and hard work to pay off. Change can't happen overnight, so don't expect it to happen this way. Instead, your goal should be to develop the skills needed, so you feel ready to face any challenges your mental health throws at you! Be patient, and start small with your goals. Start by simply just paying attention to your thoughts when you feel a negative emotion. Set yourself up for small victories that will build you the confidence to start aiming for bigger goals. Be proud of any changes you begin to make even if they are small. Have patience with yourself, and try to recognize that progress isn't necessarily linear. You may have a more challenging time at a particular stage of CBT but an easier time during other stages.

- Be kind and gentle to yourself.

When suffering from mental health disorders, it is easy to get wrapped up in your negative self-talk without realizing it. However, continually feeling negative will not generate the confidence required to help yourself get better. Try to notice your negative thoughts like "Why do I never do anything right?" or "Other people don't struggle with this!" and replace these thoughts with something less harsh. Before you start judging yourself, ask yourself if your friend or family is in the same situation as you and having these thoughts, what would you say? Try to replace the ideas you have about yourself with the thoughts you would have towards other people. Doing this sounds easy to do, but the hard part is catching yourself when you fall into a negative spiral of self-judgment. Keep in mind that this doesn't mean you should be making excuses for yourself if you did make a mistake. However, this means that you should encourage yourself to stop the harsh self-judgment that you wouldn't use for other people.

- Do things that you love.

Mental disorders like anxiety and depression have a nasty way of stripping you away from things that you enjoy in life. Usually, it is because you have become scared of the possibility of failing at them or simply just lacking the motivation to pursue them. It could be as simple as having a love for reading, but you are too tired to do so. Make an active effort to schedule in time to do the things you love. While doing the things you love, try to make sure that you are being present and paying attention at the moment instead of letting your mind worry about the future or the past. Once you finish doing something that you love, ask yourself if it made you feel better. If so, this is a huge reason why you should be doing it regularly.

- Practice mindfulness.

In modern-day society, being mindful is a challenge due to the constant need to be doing something. You have probably experienced the feeling of laying in bed trying to go to sleep but find your mind thinking about a deadline at work or something that you said to your co-worker the other day. Regardless, these are all thoughts that are preventing you from being in the moment. Start small by trying to switch these thoughts away from events that aren't happening right now. Try asking yourself if your emotions are reflecting what is going on at that moment. If not, focus on your surroundings. Pay attention to how your body feels, the noises outside, the color of your walls. By being mindful, you are eliminating the possibility of negative automatic thoughts.

CHAPTER 3
What Can Cognitive Behavioral Therapy Treat?

Anxiety and depression are the most common disorders that people face in modern-day. The most common treatment for these disorders is Cognitive Behavioral Therapy (CBT). In addition to these two disorders, CBT can treat several other illnesses and conditions. In this chapter, we will look at the disorders that CBT can treat and how it can effectively treat them.

Psychologists originally developed CBT for the treatment of depression. Since then, CBT has been used to treat a variety of disorders in different settings. Over 250 analyses and research conducted over the last few decades, scientists found strong evidence in favor of using CBT for multiple types of mental disorders. While most of these studies focused on the adult population, some evidence supports CBT within children, adolescents, and the senior population.

What Is Depression?

You have likely heard of the term depression many times in your life. What exactly is depression? The dictionary definition of depression is *'feelings of severe despondency and dejection.'* Depression is a common buzzword and illness that people frequently talk about in the present-day. However, what does it mean? Somebody can feel 'depressed' as an emotion, but it does not necessarily mean that they have a mental disorder of depression. For starters, depression itself is also known as a major depressive disorder. It is a serious and common medical illness that affects the way people feel; it negatively affects them in most cases. Since depression heavily affects how a person feels, it also affects how they think and how they act. Luckily, depression is a treatable illness, and it is something that you can recover from using the right treatments.

Keep in mind that depression is not the same as feelings of sadness or grief. The death of a loved one or the ending of a relationship are both very difficult experiences for a person to experience and endure. It is entirely normal for feelings of sadness and grief to arise during these hard times in response to those situations. People who are experiencing an event of a loss might often describe themselves as being 'depressed.'

With that said, being sad is not the same as having the disorder of depression. A person's grieving process is unique to every individual, but it does share many of the same feelings that a depression disorder brings. Both depression and grief feelings involve feelings of sadness and withdrawal from a person's usual activities. Here are a few important ways that they are different:
- When a person is feeling emotions of grief, their painful feelings often come in waves. They usually mix with positive memories

about the person who's passed. When a person is feeling intense grief, their interest and mood decrease for around two weeks.
- When a person is in grief, their self-esteem usually does not change much. When a person has depression, they have constant feelings of self-loathing and worthlessness.
- For most people, the death of a loved one can cause major depression. For other people, it could be losing their job or being a victim of physical assault. When depression and grief are co-existing, the grief is usually the more painful feeling and lasts longer than grief without depression. There is some overlap between depression and despair, but despite this, they are still different. Helping a person distinguish between grief and depression is necessary to help them get help, support, or treatment.

Symptoms of Depression

One of the most essential parts of learning about how CBT can treat depression is first learning about the symptoms of depression. Understanding which symptoms depression causes can help people identify the difference between a period of grieving to an actual depression disorder. When a person feels sad, has negative thoughts, or has trouble sleeping, it does not necessarily mean that they have depression. For a person to be diagnosed with a depression disorder, they must be exhibiting these traits:
- The person's symptoms must be new to them or be noticeably worse compared to how they were before the depressive episode
- The person's symptoms must persist for most of the day and be as consistent as nearly every day for at least two consecutive weeks
- The episode that this person experiences also comes with impaired functioning or clinically significant distress

When you suspect that you may have a depression disorder, it is extremely important to discuss ALL of the symptoms you may be experiencing. The goal of depression treatments is to help people feel more like themselves again to enjoy the things they used to do. Professionals must find the right treatment to alleviate and address all their symptoms to achieve this peace of mind. Even if a person's doctor prescribes them medication suitable for their type of depression, this may take quite a bit of time. Some people must try different medicines until they find one that works best for their specific body. The goal of depression treatment is not only about getting better from it but also about staying better.

Throughout this book, we have to remember that depression is not a simple change of mood or a moment of 'weakness.' depression is a real medical condition that has many behavioral, physical, emotional, and cognitive symptoms. We will begin talking about all the different types of depression symptoms.

Emotional Symptoms

The most common symptoms of depression are emotional symptoms. These symptoms are the ones where you feel is affecting your state of mind. Here are examples of a few emotional symptoms that people with depression have to endure:

- **Constant sadness:** This symptom is the feeling of sorrow in a depressed person for no apparent reason. This feeling can feel very intense. It often feels like nothing can make it go away.
- **Feeling of worthlessness:** A person that is depressed often experiences unrealistic feelings of worthlessness or guilt. Usually, there isn't a specific event that provokes these feelings; they just happen at random.
- **Suicidal or dark thoughts:** These types of thoughts can occur very frequently during a person's depression. Therapists and professionals take these thoughts very seriously, and when a person is experiencing these emotions, they must ask for help right away.
- **Loss of interest or pleasure in activities that you previously enjoyed:** A depressed person may experience a loss of interest that affects all areas of their life. The loss of interest can range from not finding pleasure from their previous hobbies to everyday activities that the person used to enjoy.

Physical Symptoms

Physical symptoms play a considerable role in a person's depression. Usually, when people experience physical symptoms, they are close to discovering that they may have depression. Many people think that depression is limited to emotional symptoms, but this is untrue. Here are a few physical symptoms of depression:

- **Low energy:** People who have depression typically always feel low on energy even if they have not exerted themselves. This type of depressive fatigue is different because neither sleep nor rest can alleviate this tiredness.
- **Psychomotor impairment:** Depression can make a person feel as if everything slows down. This slowing includes slowed speech, body movement, thinking, speech in low volume, long pauses before answering, inflection, or muteness.
- **Aches and pains:** Depression can often cause physical pain. This pain includes joint pain, stomach pain, headaches, back pain, or other pains).
- **Insomnia or hypersomnia:** When a person is depressed, their sleep becomes broken and feels unrefreshing. When the person

wakes up, they are usually in a mental anguish that prevents them from falling back to sleep. Other cases can be the opposite where the person is excessively sleeping.
- **Change in weight:** A change in a person's weight is a significant sign for diagnosing depression.

Behavioral Symptoms

Besides emotional and physical symptoms, behavioral symptoms also play a considerable role in diagnosing depression. Some behavioral symptoms include:
- **Change in appetite:** The most common of all behavioral symptoms of depression is a decrease in appetite. People with depression report that food seems tasteless, and they think all servings are too large. Consequently, some people increase their food consumption instead, especially sweet foods, resulting in weight gain.
- **The impression of restlessness:** For some people, depression makes them very jumpy and agitated. They may struggle with sitting still, not pacing, fiddling with items, or hand-wringing.

Cognitive Symptoms

Cognitive symptoms are one of the least talked about symptoms when it comes to depression. This one is hard to diagnose, as many people don't know if they are experiencing it. The main cognitive symptom of depression is as follows:
- **Difficulty making decisions or focusing:** A depressed person may experience a lower ability to concentrate or think. This lowered concentration causes them to exhibit behaviors of indecisiveness.

Types of Depression

As we mentioned earlier, depression is different for everyone, and therefore, different people require different treatment methods. Depression isn't just one size fits all; it is a disorder that comes in many shapes and forms. When people get diagnosed with depression, doctors will define its severity by determining where its mild, moderate, or major. Determining this can be a complicated task, but knowing what type of depression you have can help you manage your symptoms and help you find the most effective depression to your specific type of depression. Let's learn about a few different types:

Mild and Moderate Depression

The most common types of depression are mild and moderate depression. This type of depression is more than just feeling 'sad' or 'blue' the symptoms of this type of depression often interferes with people's lives by robbing them of motivation and joy. These symptoms can feel amplified in moderate depression and often lower a person's self-esteem and self-confidence.

A type of 'low-grade' depression is called dysthymia. When a person has dysthymia, they feel mild to moderately depressed more often than not, but they do have brief periods of feeling a normal mood. Here are some defining traits of dysthymia:

- Symptoms of dysthymia are not as severe or strong as the symptoms of major depression, but they do tend to last for a long time (minimum of 2 years)
- Some people report that they experience intense depressive episodes on top of having dysthymia; this is a condition called 'double depression.'
- When a person is suffering from dysthymia, they may feel like they have always been depressed for their whole lives. They may think that their consistent low mood is 'just the way they are.'

Major Depression

Major depression is a less common form of mild or moderate depression; it involves severe and relentless symptoms. Here are two characteristics of major depression:

- If major depression is left untreated, it usually lasts for about six months
- Although some people only experience one depressive episode in their life, major depression can be a disorder that is recurring throughout their life

Atypical Depression

Atypical depression is a subtype of major depression that is very common that has specific symptom patterns. It has a better response with some medications and therapies than others, identifying this type of depression is very helpful when it comes to prescribing treatment. Here are a few traits to describe it further:

- Usually, atypical depression experiences a temporary increase in mood as a response to positive events. This increase in mood includes hanging out with friends or receiving some sort of good news.
- Atypical depression includes increased appetite, weight gain, sleeping excessively, sensitivity to rejection, and a 'heavy feeling' in their arms and legs.

Seasonal Affective Disorder (SAD)

Although many people think this type of depression is just a myth, it is a real condition. When they experience reduced daylight hours during winter, some people can cause them to form a type of depression called seasonal affective disorder (SAD). Although this is not a popular type of depression, SAD affects 1% - 2% of the general population, predominantly young people and women. SAD can make a person feel completely different from the person they are in the summer. People tend to feel stressed, sad, hopeless, tense, and have little interest in friends or activities they normally enjoy. SAD usually begins during Autumn or Winter, where the days are short and remains until Spring's brighter days come along.

The Science of Depression

One of the most important things for treating their depression is to get a very thorough understanding of it. Otherwise, they may blame their depression on other unhealthy factors, like their physical appearance, personality, social life, or lack of it. There are many theories behind what causes depression, but due to extensive research, this condition is mostly due to complex individual factors; the most widely accepted theory behind it is irregular brain chemistry.

Those who suffer from depression sometimes can relate their illness to a specific circumstance or event, for instance, something traumatic that has happened to them. However, it is also not unusual for people to wonder why they are depressed because they feel as if they don't have a reason to be. In both these cases, learning about the science and theories behind depression can help understand their version of depression.

Researchers in this field have theorized that for some people, depression can be caused by having not enough substances such as neurotransmitters in the human brain, and this can cause depression. Restoring some of these brain chemicals and finding a healthy balance can alleviate some people's depression symptoms. This balance is where medication such as antidepressants come in. We will discuss the different classes and types of antidepressants later on in this book.

This theory seems to be the simplest to tackle. I mean, it's just a matter of biology, math, and prescription that can get someone back on track, right? Wrong. Although it does seem simple, depression is an extremely complex condition to treat. Just because a person successfully treated their depression using medication, it doesn't mean that the next person can find success with the same method. Even a treatment method for someone who has worked successfully may slowly begin lower in effectiveness over time or even stop working completely. This lowered effectiveness happens for numerous reasons that scientists are still trying to comprehend. Researchers are still heavily invested in this area of science to continue to understand the mechanisms of depression more deeply, including chemicals in our brains, with the hope of finding more explanations and evidence for these complexities to continue developing more treatment methods for people.

Depression is still a multifaceted condition. However, simply having knowledge or awareness of the chemistry component in a person's brain proves to be very useful for mental health and medical professionals, and people suffering from depressive disorders. Below is a summary of the recognized science behind a depression disorder:

Neurotransmitters

For simplicity's sake, the chemical 'messengers' in our brain are called neurotransmitters. The nerve cells within our brain use these messengers, aka neurotransmitters, to communicate with one another. We believe that the messages that they send play a huge role in a person's mood regulation. The three neurotransmitters that are responsible for depression are:
- Dopamine
- Serotonin
- Norepinephrine

Besides these neurotransmitters, others also send messages in a person's brain. These include; GABA, acetylcholine, and glutamate. Scientists are still studying the specifics of what role these chemicals play in the brain when it comes to a person's depression or other mental conditions like fibromyalgia and Alzheimer's.

Let's learn a little about how our cells communicate with our neurotransmitters. A synapse is a space between two nerve cells. When two cells want to communicate with each other, our neurotransmitters can be packed up and then released from the cell for the destined cell to receive. As these packaged neurotransmitters travel across space, postsynaptic cells can take up those receptors to look for a specific chemical. For instance, serotonin receptors will aim to pick up serotonin molecules. If there are any excess lingering molecules in that space, the presynaptic cell will gather them and use them in another communication by reprocessing them. Different types of neurotransmitters carry different messages that play a specific role in creating a person's brain chemistry. Imbalanced in those chemicals are theorized to play a huge role in depression or other mental health conditions.

- Norepinephrine

Norepinephrine plays a dual purpose as a neurotransmitter and hormone. It is responsible for the 'fight or flight' response that humans feel, including adrenaline. It helps deliver messages between cells. In the 60s, scientists suggested that the chemical of interest was norepinephrine when it came to the human brain and depression. These scientists proposed "catecholamine" as the hypothesis of all mood disorders. They suggested that when there isn't enough norepinephrine in the human brain, that was when depression occurred. Otherwise, manic disorders occur when a person's brain has too much norepinephrine. Although there is plenty of evidence that supports this statement, many other researchers have challenged it. Firstly, they discovered that changes in norepinephrine levels do not affect every person's mood. Also, depression can be alleviated in some people by changing the levels of norepinephrine. Ultimately, researchers in the present-day now understand that low levels of norepinephrine are not the only chemical-cause of depression.

- Serotonin

Serotonin is one of the most well-known chemicals in the general population. Almost everybody knows that serotonin is the 'feel-good' chemical in a person's brain. Not only does serotonin help regulate a person's mood, but it also has a variety of different jobs in the human body ranging from blood clotting to sexual function. As it relates to depression, researchers have focused their time and efforts on serotonin over the past 20 years. This research has led to the invention of antidepressants like Prozac or other SSRIs, which is known as selective serotonin reuptake inhibitors. Just like the name SSRI states, these types of medication focus on acting upon serotonin molecules. A few famous doctors originally proposed that low levels of serotonin cause norepinephrine drop as well. Still, serotonin levels can be manipulated through the use of medication to raise norepinephrine. Another type of antidepressant, known as *Tricyclic antidepressants* (TCAs), can also affect serotonin and norepinephrine. However, they affect histamine and acetylcholine as well. TCAs' side effects include dry eyes, dry mouth, sensitivity to light, peculiar taste in the mouth, blurry vision, urinary hesitancy, and constipation. Consequently, SSRIs do not affect acetylcholine and histamine levels and don't offer TCAs' same side effects. Due to this, doctors and depressed people tend to opt for TCAs or different classes of antidepressants.

- Dopamine

The third chemical that has a huge role in a person's mood is dopamine. The chemical dopamine is also very well known, and people know that it is responsible for happiness and mood. Positive feelings related to reinforcement and reward are created by dopamine, helping people stay motivated to continue doing an activity or task. Scientists also believe that dopamine plays a big role in numerous conditions that involve the brain, including schizophrenia and Parkinson's. There is evidence that shows that lower dopamine levels contribute to depression in some people. When people go through many treatments that fail, doctors have prescribed medications that act like dopamine and found success. However, keep in mind that most medications used for depression usually take 6+ weeks to be effective. In our present-day, researchers are also focusing on finding out whether dopamine agents in medication can produce a faster result for treating depression. However, we must consider that there are a few severe disadvantages when using dopamine as medication. Dopamine is also encouraged to be produced by recreational drugs such as alcohol, opiates, and cocaine. It is not unheard of for people to self-medicate when they are depressed by using these substances. When someone activates their dopamine reward cycle through substance use, they can develop addictions as a result.

- Low Neurotransmitter Levels

Since we understand low levels of neurotransmitters cause depression, then our next question is, what exactly are the causes of low levels of norepinephrine, dopamine, or serotonin to begin with? Recent research has found a few potential causes of chemical imbalances in a person's brain. These causes could include:

- Not enough receptor sites available to receive neurotransmitters
- Not enough of a specific neurotransmitter is producing
- Not enough molecules that are responsible for building neurotransmitters
- Presynaptic cells are taking the neurotransmitters back up before it has the opportunity to be received by the destined cell
- The molecules that are responsible for making neurotransmitters are running out

An interruption anywhere in the total process can result in lower levels of neurotransmitters. Numerous new theories focus on the factors that cause low levels, for instance, mitochondrial stress. One of the main difficulties that doctors and researchers have in connecting low levels of brain chemicals to depression is that no method can consistently and accurately measure this. Other parts of the human body are also responsible for making neurotransmitters. These amounts need to be measured and considered when it comes to diagnosing depression and when looking for the most effective treatment method.

How Can CBT Be Used to Treat Depression

There is strong evidence that supports the use of CBT to treat depression at a moderate level. However, there isn't strong evidence that supports CBT as a treatment for more severe depression. The evidence for severe depression is mixed, but some studies suggest that CBT is as effective as medication.

That being said; however, CBT does still perform better for moderate depression compared to no treatment at all. Further, it performs better than other pharmaceutical or behavioral therapies. CBT is effective when it comes to preventing relapses as well.

As I mentioned, depression is a very complex disorder, and it reacts differently in each person that experiences it. There are also several different types of depression, as we saw above. For this reason, CBT is best used in combination with other treatment methods when it comes to treating depression. Each person should seek treatment and a therapist or doctor to find the treatment that works best for their case of depression.

What Is Anxiety?

The next disorder that CBT is effective in treating is anxiety. You have likely heard this work before, but what exactly is anxiety?

Often, when people use the term 'anxiety,' they are referring to generalized anxiety. Anxiety is a basic feeling and experience that every species of animal experiences. Although anxiety is not a pleasant feeling, it is not dangerous. Anxiety is helpful for us in certain situations. We all have to keep in mind that anxiety is a normal emotion and not dangerous. The symptoms of anxiety serve a function. Anxiety is a natural reaction to a perceived threat and helps us humans respond to it. However, if you have excessive anxiety, it can also be a problem.

The Most Common Causes of Anxiety

As you have just learned, a lot of the time, having one anxiety disorder can lead to a higher risk of developing others. Let's use OCD as an example. An individual suffering from OCD often feels a lot of shame and secrecy when it comes to their compulsive tendencies. A lot of the time, they don't want to showcase their tendencies around other people. This need to hide then creates a fear of being around other people. Having a fear of interacting and being around others is also a sign of a social disorder. If one anxiety disorder is left untreated for long periods, those symptoms will likely snowball into other ones.

All anxiety disorders have one thing in common; worry. Since worry is the largest component of anxiety and is responsible for generating anxiety, if someone is unable to manage their worry - they will likely become anxious and exhibit anxious behaviors. The worry that causes someone to develop GAD is the same worry that can cause someone to develop panic disorders. When someone is dealing with an overwhelming amount of worry, their environmental factors play a part in determining what type of disorder it manifests into. For instance, let's use two Bob and John as examples. Bob and John both experience the same amount of worry. Bob grew up in an environment where his parents exhibited excessive cleaning behaviors. John grew up in an environment where he was timid and never learned how to break out of his shyness. Assuming Bob and John are facing the same amount of worry is equal, Bob is likely to develop an obsessive-compulsive disorder because of his exposure to his parents' cleaning tendencies. However, John is likely to develop social anxiety disorder due to his childhood and the lack of help to work through his timid personality.

The common factor in anxiety disorders is the worry, which then manifests into anxiety. Environmental factors affect what these anxieties become, which affects what their behavior will be. As we discussed earlier, those suffering from one anxiety disorder may develop another one if they don't treat the first within a reasonable time frame.

A common question that is asked often in modern-day society is, 'Is there an anxiety epidemic?" It seems like everywhere we go, and everyone we know is battling some sort of anxiety disorder. Media outlets are constantly talking about depression and anxiety, and chances are, a significant portion of people we know are using medication to battle their anxiety disorder(s). Are we being affected by the same forms of anxiety as our ancestors? The answer is that the way that anxiety manifests itself in people hasn't changed over time. We are still affected by the same forms of anxiety that affected our ancestors. However, the things that did change about anxiety are the triggers that we face. The traditional causes of anxieties that humans face are still prevalent today. For example, we still experience anxiety due to difficult relationships, bad health, poverty, disadvantage, and unemployment. Some of these traditional sources of anxiety are at an increase in the present day. These sources include; loneliness, undesirable relationship factors like divorce, or violence and abuse, childhood neglect, increased work stress and hours, and an overwhelming sense of lack of control over our lives. The lack of control is especially prevalent amongst the youth of our society who are being introduced to failure early on in their lives due to an increased systematic educational testing. Luckily, some of the most traditional anxiety sources, such as poverty and poor health, are on the decline. Still, it creates space for new anxieties, such as the stress of modern-day jobs and income inequality.

Moreover, modern technology and media have created an entirely new set of anxiety sources for the present generations. Yes, we are talking about social media. The need to have 24/7 connectivity, the need to multitask various activities at all times, and the need to keep up with news alerts and doomsday scenarios. Soon, almost every single appliance in our homes will have internet connectivity to grant you access to social media to keep you online. This increase in connectivity will increase the fears of data hacking, identity theft, trolling, phishing, and even grooming. Even our simple computers bring in daily anxieties that include; forgotten passwords, hard drive crashes, and daily digital transactions. All transactions start to feel very distant when they are all done through technology. A lot of the time, all you want is to just speak to a real person. Did you know that most children under the age of 20 have never lived without social media to build off of social media anxiety? The present research has associated social media use with social anxiety. The research proposes that social anxiety and loneliness can generate feelings of disconnectedness when we are constantly viewing the rich and successful lives of others. Another consequence of social media use is that the youth track their social success and status using metrics like the number of followers or friends they have on their social media. The metrics are different from the traditional way people counted how many real genuine friends they had.

On top of the numerous new and modern anxieties, there is an increasing social culture shift regarding anxiety. This change has been very contradictory in terms of the messages it sends to society. We constantly hear that anxiety is an appropriate feeling in response to the modern-day stresses. Anxiety is almost a sort of status symbol that showcases how successful and busy you are. However, we also hear that having too much anxiety requires treatment. The diagnosis of different categories of anxiety has exploded over the past thirty years. The pharmaceutical industry has never been keener to medicalize anxiety so they can sell us a pharmaceutical fix for it. This fix led to numerous social campaigns over the years to bring awareness to mental health disorders (e.g., depression and anxiety) to destigmatize it, diagnose it, and seek medical treatment for it.

Although our anxiety epidemic sounds dooming, it is not entirely the case. According to research, 20% of people suffer from extremely high anxiety levels, but no evidence supports the growth of this ratio. If the ratio remains at 20%, due to our population's growth, the number of people suffering from anxiety will grow too. As more people face anxiety disorders, more people will be seeking treatment for it as we continue to bring awareness to mental health. On the other hand, 40% of people experience low anxiety levels and will not be motivated to seek treatment unless they go through a very distressing event or period of their life.

The Science of Anxiety

Since anxiety is a normal response to a threat, when a person perceives that they are threatening, this triggers their fight or flight instinct. Its sole purpose is to protect itself by fighting or fleeing from danger. When somebody feels threatened, their brain sends messages to your autonomic nervous system (this is a section of your nerves). When this nervous system reacts, it releases adrenalin and noradrenalin from the brain, which then triggers the anxiety response and automatically prepares us for danger. This nervous system eventually stops when our bodies destroy these chemicals to calm the body down.

This fact is extremely important to remember because those who suffer from anxiety disorders believe that their anxiety will go on forever. However, biologically this cannot happen since the body limits anxiety over time. Although it may feel that the anxiety is going on forever, it has a limited lifespan. After some time, your body will determine that it has had enough with the fight or flight instinct and restore the body to its neutral feeling. Anxiety cannot continue endlessly or damage your body. Although highly uncomfortable, this whole cycle is perfectly harmless and natural. This behavior is instinct to us because, in the wild, it is necessary for our bodies to reactivate this response. After all, we know that danger can return.

Overall, the "fight or flight" response activates the entire body's metabolism. This response makes someone feel hot, flushed, and tired afterward because the entire process uses up a lot of energy. After a strong anxiety experience, most people feel drained, tired, and completely worn out.

Anxiety Disorders

Now that you know what anxiety is and how it is a natural emotion that we feel for protection - what is an anxiety disorder? An anxiety disorder is a medical condition where the individual feels symptoms of extreme anxiety or panic. In other words, an anxiety disorder is when the individual is feeling severe anxiety or panic and is unable to manage their symptoms.

We will be going through all the different types of anxiety disorders in another subchapter, but in this one, we will be talking about the most common ones that people face nowadays. The most common anxiety disorder that people face in the present-day is Generalized Anxiety disorder.

Symptoms of Anxiety Disorders

Diagnosing anxiety is far from simple. Unlike physical illnesses, it is not caused by a germ or bacteria that we can detect in a blood test. Anxiety manifests in numerous forms and can also be a symptom of other existing medical conditions. To properly diagnose anxiety, you need to complete a physical examination. This examination will allow your doctor to determine if other health issues cause your anxiety symptoms or if your anxiety is masking other symptoms. Usually, a complete personal health history is needed to make a complete diagnosis.

A rule of thumb is that you need to be 100% honest with the doctor making your diagnosis. Multiple things contribute to or can be affected by anxiety. These factors include:
- Hormones
- Specific Illnesses
- Coffee and/or alcohol consumption
- Medications

Certain medical conditions can also cause symptoms that appear like anxiety. Physical anxiety symptoms include:
- Shortness of breath
- Racing heart
- Sweating
- Shaking
- Chills or hot flashes

- Nausea
- Chest pain
- Vomiting
- Diarrhea
- Frequent urination
- Dry mouth

Your doctor will likely perform a variety of physical exams on you to help rule out possible medical conditions that mimic anxiety symptoms. Medical conditions that share similar symptoms with anxiety are:

- Asthma
- Heart attack
- Withdrawal related to substance abuse
- Side effects of diabetes or high blood pressure drugs
- Withdrawals from drugs used to treat sleep disorders or anxiety
- Hyperthyroidism
- Menopause
- Angina

Your doctor may suggest that you complete self-assessment questionnaires before you complete another testing after ruling out medical conditions. This assessment can help you recognize whether you have an anxiety disorder or react to a distressing event or situation. If the self-assessments result in the possibility of an anxiety disorder, your doctor may recommend you take a clinical assessment or have a structured interview with you.

Generalized Anxiety Disorder (GAD)

Generalized anxiety is the susceptibility to excessive panic, worry, or anxiety regarding numerous events or situations. Usually, the person has major difficulty controlling their feelings of worry and is associated with other symptoms such as fatigue, restlessness, concentration difficulties, sleep disturbance, irritability, and muscle tension. We define the feeling of worry as a process focused on the uncertainty of the outcome regarding future events. It is not an emotion itself, but it leads to feeling the emotion of anxiety. The main and most obvious symptom of generalized anxiety disorder is the "what if" thoughts that begin to occur. These "what if" thoughts work hand in hand with worrying, and it often feels like it is uncontrollable. Also, the process of worry is often associated with physical symptoms that are related to the flight or fight response. It often happens that the individual will think of the future negatively and have thoughts that are followed by feelings of anxiety.

People with GAD often feel worried and anxious most of the time and not just in specific stressful situations. The worries that they have been constant, intense, and interferes with their daily routine. Their worries are typically multiple aspects and not only one. It may include work, health, finance, family, or just everyday life things. Trivial tasks such as household chores or being late for a meeting can lead to extreme anxiety, leading to doom.

Most people are diagnosed with GAD if they showcase some of the symptoms for six months or more:
- You feel extremely worried about numerous activities or events.
- You struggle to stop worrying.
- You are finding that your anxiety has made it very hard for you to do your daily routine (e.g., studying, working, hanging out with friends)
- You constantly feel restless or on edge.
- You are always/easily tired.
- You struggle with concentration.
- You are easily irritable.
- You have tension in your muscles (e.g., neck or sore jaw)
- You struggle with sleeping (e.g., difficulty staying asleep or falling asleep)

About 14% of the population suffers from GAD in the present day. This condition tends to appear in more women than men and can occur at any time in an individual's life. It is common in all age groups, even including young children and seniors. However, the most common time for diagnosis is when an individual is around 30 years of age. Children who suffer from GAD will usually have exhibit behaviors like:
- Being un-confident of themselves
- Being over-conforming
- They are seeking constant approval and assurance from others.
- Being a perfectionist
- Needing to re-do tasks to perfection
- Using the phrase "Yes, but what if?"

So what exactly causes GAD? This one is tricky; there is a combination of different factors that take place. First, we consider biological factors. GAD is associated with certain changes in brain functions. Next, we also consider family history. Often, people who have GAD have a history of mental health issues in their family. Stressful life events also increase the risk of someone developing GAD. For example, loss of a relationship, moving, or physical or emotional abuse are all examples of events that can play a role in causing GAD. Lastly, psychological factors may also put a person at higher risk. Those who have personality traits of being sensitive, nervous, or inability to tolerate frustration are at higher risk of GAD.

The most common treatment for GAD is Cognitive Behavioral Therapy. You can turn to medication if psychological treatments are ineffective. We will be diving into the later chapters on why and how CBT is an extremely effective treatment for those who have GAD.

Other Types of Anxiety Disorders

Now that we have learned about the most common anxiety disorder, generalized anxiety disorder (GAD), and the largest component that leads to it (worry), we will learn about other types of anxiety disorders that people suffer from. The other types of anxiety disorders that we will learn about are:
- Social Anxiety
- Specific Phobias
- Panic Disorder
- Obsessive-Compulsive Disorder (OCD)
- Post-traumatic Stress Disorder (PTSD)

People who experience anxiety often showcase symptoms of more than one type of anxiety disorder. It's important to learn about these early on to help identify the symptoms to get treatment early on. Usually, the symptoms that you may experience do not go away on their own, and if they are left untreated, they can begin to take over your daily life.

- Social Anxiety

Although it is very normal to feel a certain level of nervousness in social situations, it is not normal to feel overwhelming anxiety. Situations such as attending formal events, public speaking, and doing presentations are likely events in which you feel nervous and anxious. However, for those who suffer from social anxicty (or otherwise known as social phobia), speaking or performing in front of other people and general social situations can lead to extreme anxiety. This anxiety usually stems from the fear of being criticized, judged, humiliated, or laughed at in front of other people. A lot of the time, they are afraid of trivial and ordinary matters. For example, those who suffer from social anxiety may feel that eating at a restaurant around other people can be extremely daunting.

Social anxiety usually occurs during the lead up to performance events (e.g., having to give a speech or working while people are watching them) and situations where social interaction is involved (e.g., having lunch with coworkers or normal small talk). Social anxiety also occurs during the actual event and the lead-up. Moreover, this type of phobia can also be very specific where the individual fears a specific situation. For example, they can be fearful of having to be assertive during work meetings.

The symptoms of social anxiety include psychological and physical symptoms. People with social phobia find it very distressing when they experience physical symptoms. These physical symptoms include:
- Excessive perspiration
- Nausea/Diarrhea
- Trembling
- Stammering, stuttering, or blushing when speaking

When these physical symptoms occur, it normally causes the anxiety to increase as the person begins to fear that other people will notice these signs. However, these signs are usually not noticeable to other people. Those who suffer from this condition say that they also excessively worry that they will say or do something wrong, which will lead to a terrible result. Often, people with social anxiety will attempt to avoid situations where they feel like they can act in an embarrassing or humiliating way. If they can't avoid certain situations, they will choose to endure it but will become very distressed and anxious and try to exit that situation as fast as possible. This enduring can begin to harm their relationships. Moreover, it may begin to affect their professional lives and their ability to maintain their daily routine.

We base a typical social anxiety diagnosis on having the symptoms mentioned above and how much distress and impairment it causes on the individual's day-to-day routine. Usually, if symptoms continue for six months or more, then the doctor will make a diagnosis.

Some social phobia symptoms that are psychological include:
- They are feeling extreme nervousness before performing in front of other people.
- They are feeling extreme nervousness before meeting unfamiliar people.
- They are feeling extreme nervousness or embarrassment when being observed (e.g., eating or drinking in front of others, talking on the phone in front of others)
- They are not going to certain events or interactions due to the fear of social nervousness.
- They are having difficulty going about daily life (e.g., studying, seeing friends, and working)

Research suggests that 11% of the population has experienced social anxiety in their lifetime. It showed that women experience this disorder more than men. A lot of the time, this phobia starts during childhood or adolescence.

So, what exactly causes social anxiety? There are numerous causes, but the most common ones are temperament, family history, and learned behavior. When it comes to temperament, children or adolescents who are shy are at more risk than others. Specifically, for children, those who exhibit shyness and timidity puts them at risk of developing social anxiety in their adulthood. Family history is also a possibility when it comes to cause due to genetic predisposition. The leading cause, however, is usually learned behavior. Often, those who suffer from social anxiety develop this condition due to being treated poorly, embarrassed in public, or humiliated.

When it comes to treating social phobia, psychological treatments will be the first line of treatment, and in more severe cases, medication can be effective. Since social phobia is a type of anxiety disorder, many professionals choose to use Cognitive Behavioral Therapy as a treatment method. Later on in this book, we will be talking about how CBT helps treat anxiety disorders.

- Phobias

Phobias are probably one of the most well-known disorders that we hear about in present-day society. You probably see people on TV and movies that have phobias of clowns, spiders, or heights. Fear or concern regarding certain situations is common, but that does not mean you have a phobia. Feeling anxious when you come across a spider or being in a high place is relatively normal. Fear is a rational and natural response when we are in situations where we feel threatened.

However, some people have a huge reaction to certain activities, situations, or objects due to them imagining and exaggerating the danger. The feelings of terror, panic, or fear that someone may feel due to a threat are entirely out of proportion. In many cases, even a thought of the phobic stimulus or seeing it on TV is enough to cause a reaction in these individuals. These types of extreme reactions could indicate a specific phobia disorder.

Although people are not self-aware of where their anxiety is coming from, people who suffer from phobias are usually aware that their fears are irrational and extreme. However, they do feel that their reactions are automatic and that they cannot control them. Sometimes, specific phobias lead to panic attacks. During these panic attacks, the individual finds themselves overwhelmed with undesirable physical sensations. These sensations include nausea, heart racing, choking, chest pain, dizziness, faintness, and hot/cold flashes.

The symptoms of specific phobia are as follows:

- You have a constant, extreme, and irrational fear of a situation, activity, or object. For example, you have a fear of heights, clowns, or spiders.
- You are constantly avoiding situations where there is a possibility that you have to face your phobia—for example, not going outside because you may encounter a spider. If the situation is difficult to avoid, you may start to feel high levels of distress.
- You find that your avoidance and anxiety of certain situations where your phobia might exist makes it hard for you to go about your daily routine. For example, it begins to interfere with your work, school, or social life.
- You find that your avoidance and anxiety are constant, and you have been struggling with it for over six months.

We can split specific phobias into the following categories:

- Animals: Your fear is related to animals or insects (e.g., fear of cats or spiders)
- Natural environment: Your fear is related to the natural environment (e.g., fear of heights or lightning)
- Injury/injection: Your fear is related to invasive medical procedures (e.g., fear of needles or seeing blood)
- Situations: Your fear is related to very specific situations (e.g., riding an escalator or driving in heavy traffic)
- Other: Your fear is to over miscellaneous phobias (e.g., fear of throwing up or fear of choking)

The first sign of specific phobia symptoms usually come up during childhood or early adolescence. Fear is quite normal amongst children, and they experience a lot of common fears during their childhood. Common fears are; being afraid of strangers, imaginary monsters, the dark, and animals. However, learning to manage these fears properly is part of the process of growing up. Some children can still develop specific phobias to the severity of panic attacks. These children have a higher risk to develop specific phobias compared to the other types of anxiety disorders. In most cases, children are not aware of the fact that their fears are extreme and irrational.

So, what exactly causes specific phobias besides anxiety? Like social anxiety, a person's temperament and history of mental health conditions play a huge role in the causation of specific phobias. Phobias are very treatable, and we use psychological treatments like CBT first to tackle the disorder. In cases where specific phobia is more severe, medication will be involved to help with the disorder.

- Panic Disorder

Panic disorder, or more commonly known as 'panic attacks,' is the term used to describe when these attacks are recurring and disabling. Usually, panic disorders are defined by:
- Unexpected and recurring panic attacks.
- You worry for a long duration (1 month+) after having a panic attack that you will have another one.
- You are worried about the effects or consequences after that panic attack. A lot of people will think that a panic attack is a symptom of an undiagnosed medical issue. For instance, individuals may do repeated medical tests due to these worries, and although nothing shows up, they still are afraid of being in poor health.
- You have significant behavior changes linked to the panic attacks—for example, avoiding exercise because your heart rate will increase.

Usually, during a panic attack, you become overwhelmed with the physical feelings described above. The panic attack peak is usually 10 minutes in and will last up to 30 minutes and leave you exhausted afterward. They can occur up to numerous times a day or a few times per

year. They can happen when someone is sleeping, which will wake them up during the attack. Many people have experienced a panic attack at least one time in their lives. Up to 40% of the human population has experienced a panic attack at some point in their lives. This statistic does not mean you have a panic disorder. Here are the common symptoms and signs of a panic attack:
- A feeling of overwhelming fear or panic
- You have the thought that you are choking, dying, or 'going crazy.'
- Heart rate increases
- Having difficulty breathing (e.g., hyperventilating)
- Feeling like you are choking, or your lungs aren't working.
- Perspiring excessively
- Light-headedness, dizziness, or faintness

In some cases, a person going through a panic attack can also experience 'dissociation' or 'derealisation.' This is the sensation where you feel like the world and the environment around you is not real. This symptom is associated with the intense physiological changes in the body during this anxiety attack.

Panic disorders are not as common as other disorders such as GAD or social anxiety. Shockingly, 5% of the population have experienced panic disorder within their lifetime. According to statistics, women are more prone to a panic disorder than men. Panic disorders typically occur when people are in their early to mid-20s or in their mid-life. Panic disorders can occur at any age, but they are extremely rare in children or older people.

So what exactly causes a panic disorder? Although there isn't a specific cause, multiple factors are usually involved. Included could be people with a family history of anxiety disorders or depression. Some studies even suggest that genetics plays a big role. Biological factors are also associated with panic disorders such as; asthma, irritable bowel syndrome (IBS), and hyperthyroidism. Negative experiences in life also play a huge role in panic disorders. Severely stressful life experiences like sexual abuse or bereavement sometimes lead to panic disorders. Moreover, individuals going through extreme ongoing stress are at a high risk of developing panic disorders.

When it comes to treatments for panic disorders, the treatments reduce panic attacks from those who suffer from it. We give those suffering from severe panic disorder medication to help calm them, but psychological treatments like CBT will be the first method used.

- Obsessive-Compulsive Disorder (OCD)

As we discussed in our subchapter about worry, worrying thoughts can lead to anxiety, influencing our behavior. This influence can be helpful at times. For example, thinking that you may have left your stove on will lead you to check on it to ensure you are keeping things safe. However, if that thought becomes recurring and obsessive, it begins to influence unhealthy behavior patterns that cause the daily routine to be difficult. An example of OCD is repeatedly checking the stove to make sure they turned it off, even though you have already confirmed it the first time.

Often, people who suffer from OCD feel extreme shame about their need to carry out their compulsive actions. These feelings of shame cause secrecy, which then leads to delayed diagnosis and treatment. It can often result in a social disability where children fail to go to school or adults failing to leave their homes.

So, what are the signs and symptoms of Obsessive-Compulsive Disorder? OCD usually occurs in different types:

- Cleanliness and Order: Examples include obsessive household cleaning or hand-washing to mitigate the fear of contamination or germs, obsession with symmetry or order, and an excessive need to place objects or perform tasks in a specific pattern or place.
- Counting and Hoarding: Examples include repeatedly counting objects such as bricks on the wall, counting their clothes, or hoarding useless items like old newspapers or garbage.
- Safety: This is an obsessive fear about harm occurring to loved ones or themselves and can lead to impulsively checking on things to make sure they have turned everything off, and entrances are locked.
- Sexual Issues: Having an irrational fear or disgust regarding any sexual activity.
- Religious and Moral Issues: Feeling the need or compulsion to pray numerous times a day to the point where it affects their relationships and work.

When it comes to symptoms of OCD, beware of looking out for:

- Having repetitive concerns or thoughts that are about more than just regular life problems (e.g., having thoughts that something will harm your loved ones or that something will harm you)
- Doing the same activity in a very ordered and repeated manner each time. Examples include:
    - You constantly shower, brush your teeth, wash your clothes, or your hands.
    - You constantly rearrange tidy or clean things in a particular way at home or at work.
    - You constantly check that you locked all entrances and that you turned off all electronics.
- You feel relieved after doing those tasks but soon after feeling the need to repeat them.
- Being aware that these feelings, behaviors, and tendencies are unreasonable cannot help it.

- You are finding that these behaviors and thoughts interfered with your daily routine and took up more than one hour a day.

OCD is not as common as the other disorders we have discussed. Only around 3% of the population has experienced OCD in their lifetime. OCD can occur at any stage in your lifetime, and even children as young as six years old may showcase symptoms. However, symptoms only develop fully when the individual reaches their adolescence.

Based on research, we theorize OCD to have developed from a mix of environmental factors and genetics. Multiple other factors can increase the risk of developing OCD, including social factors, psychological factors, and family history. We link biological factors such as neurological issues and irregular levels of serotonin to OCD. There is active research right now regarding how structural, chemical, and functional changes in the brain may lead to OCD. Also, learned behaviors and environmental factors can cause OCD to develop. It can happen through direct conditioning or watching the behaviors of others. Since children are very impressionable, they will have a higher risk of developing OCD in their adolescence by watching their parents' compulsive behaviors.

OCD is usually treated by psychological treatments like CBT first, but we also use medication because many cases are more severe. In certain cases, a combination of medication and psychological treatments like therapy will be used at the same time to increase effectiveness.

- Post-Traumatic Stress Disorder (PTSD)

People who have been through a traumatic situation or event that has threatened their safety, life, or the life of others can develop a set of undesirable reactions called PTSD. These traumatic situations could be anything from a car accident to war to natural disasters like an earthquake. As a result of these traumatic events, the person will have intense horror, fear, or helplessness.

Individuals who have PTSD will often have feelings of intense fear or panic, very similar to those they felt during that traumatic situation. There are four main types of difficulties within PTSD:
- Re-living the traumatic situation/event: The individual constantly re-lives the traumatic situation or event through memories; often, this takes place in the form of imagery and nightmares. This re-living can also lead to extreme physical and emotional reactions like panic, heart palpitations, or sweating.
- Being extremely alert: The individual experiences concentration issues, irritability, and insomnia. They are easily scared and startled and are always looking out for signs of danger.
- Avoiding reminders of the situation/event: The individual purposely avoids places, activities, people, emotions, or thoughts related to the traumatic event because they bring back distressing memories.

- Feeling emotionally numb: This individual has lost interest in daily activities, feels isolated from family and friends, or feeling emotionally numb.

It is quite common for people who have PTSD also to experience other types of anxiety disorder. These other disorders could have been developed as a response to the traumatic event or developed after PTSD itself. The common additional disorders that this individual may face include depression, GAD, and drug or alcohol abuse.

If someone has gone through a traumatic event that involved injury, abuse, torture, or death, then they may experience the following symptoms of PTSD:

- Flashbacks of memories or dreams of the event
- If reminded of the event, you become physically and psychologically distressed.
- You have trouble remembering significant parts of that event.
- You have a negative perspective on yourself or other people.
- You constantly blame yourself or other people for that event.
- You constantly feel the emotions of anger, guilt, or shame.
- You no longer have an interest in the things you used to enjoy
- You feel like you are cutting yourself off from other people.
- You struggle with feeling positive emotions, such as excitement or love.
- You struggle with sleeping (e.g., insomnia or nightmares)
- You are easily angered or irritated.
- You find yourself engaging in recklessness and self-destructive behavior.
- You struggle with concentrating.
- You are always alert or vigilant.
- You get startled easily.

If someone feels more than four symptoms above for a month or more, they likely have PTSD. PTSD is something that anyone can develop following a traumatic event. However, those at greater risk are normally involved in deliberate harm like physical or sexual assault. Besides the event itself, other factors of developing PTSD include having a history of mental health problems, an ongoing stressful life, or lack of social support.

Around 12% of the population has experienced PTSD in their lifetime. In the western world, serious accidents are the leading causes of PTSD. If you are someone who has just gone through a traumatic event and is feeling very distressed, start by talking to your family doctor to get diagnosed. The earlier that you implement treatment, the more effective it is in helping you.

When it comes to PTSD treatment, many people recover on their own or through friends and family support. Due to this statistic, medical treatment doesn't usually begin until at least two weeks after the traumatic event. Although formal treatment is usually not offered right away, it is important that the first few days following the event that you go to and seek help and support. The support from family and friends is crucial for most people going through trauma. Minimizing other stressful life events helps the individual focus more of their time and effort on their recovery. Treatments for PTSD usually start with psychological treatment, such as talking therapies like CBT. In some severe cases, medication will be prescribed but are usually not recommended with PTSD.

How Can CBT Treat Anxiety Disorders?
Most of the research and practices to date support the use of CBT for the treatment of anxiety. CBT is very effective in treating anxiety disorders such as; social anxiety, generalized anxiety, and PTSD. It is also proven to be effective for less common disorders such as phobias and OCD. The National Institute for Health and Care Excellence (NICE) recommends Cognitive Behavioral Therapy to be the first approach to treating anxiety disorders.

CBT has been introduced to numerous countries and has established successful programs. However, even with the newest treatments, we are still a long way from helping 100% of people recover from mental disorders. Disorders such as GAD and OCD can be lifelong debilitating conditions. GAD and OCD are very resistant in some cases, even when exposed to medications and multiple psychotherapies. The only way to help more people who are suffering from anxiety disorders is to keep funding research to refining and developing therapies.

Some people wish to get rid of anxiety completely, but that goal isn't possible or realistic! When it comes to Cognitive Behavioral Therapy, the approach is to help you build the skills required to help you manage and understand your anxiety instead of getting rid of it altogether (again, not possible).

- Stress-Related Disorders

The most harmful type of stress is chronic stress. When it is left untreated for an extended amount of time, chronic stress can cause damage that can damage your physical and mental health irreversibly. For instance, poor work environments, long-term poverty, unemployment, repeated abuse in any form, dysfunctional family, or an unhappy marriage can cause a person significant chronic stress. When a person feels hopeless and does not see any way out of it and gives up entirely on finding solutions, chronic stress can set in and begin affecting their physical and mental health. When a person continuously lives with chronic stress, their emotional and behavioral actions can become ingrained. The wiring of their brains and bodies begins to change and makes them more prone to the negative effects that stress has on a person's body regardless of what's happening to them.

Types of Stress

Chronic stress is a grinding type of stress because it wears people down day after day. It negatively impacts the body and mind significantly and has the power to change a person forever. Chronic stress can be so dangerous that it can kill people due to suicide, heart attacks, strokes, and even cancer. There are treatment practices that can help people manage their chronic stress, but it requires them to be actively practicing those techniques throughout their lives. Later in this book, we will be exploring numerous treatment methods for stress disorders and related disorders caused by stress. If you think you are someone that is suffering from chronic stress, get help right away. Seek professional opinion and get it diagnosed; that will be the first step in discovering what methods are most suitable for your type of stress.

In some cases, you may not even have chronic stress and just another type of stress. In that case, you can use different methods and techniques to manage them properly. Next up in this chapter, we will be looking at the general symptoms of stress. This section will help you identify whether or not you feel like you have a stress disorder.

Symptoms of Stress

- Acne
- Headaches
- Chronic Pain
- Frequent Sickness
- Insomnia
- Decreased Energy
- Decreased Libido
- Digestive Issues
- Appetite Changes
- Depression
- Rapid Heartbeat
- Sweating

How CBT Can Help With Stress-Related Disorders

When a person is under a lot of stress for an extended amount of time, it increases their risk of developing other mental disorders. Common disorders that can be caused by high stress include; anxiety, depression, anger disorders, and panic disorders. We have already discussed several of these disorders in this chapter, and how CBT can treat them. It is important to note that if you are under high stress, learning what disorders chronic stress can lead to may help you identify it or learn to cope with your struggles related to stress.

How CBT Can Help With Other Disorders

As you know, CBT teaches a person to look within themselves and understand themselves better.

Several types of emotional deficiencies or causes can lead a person to develop disordered mental processes, resulting in various mental health disorders. We will explore some of these factors in hopes that you will recognize some of the reasons why you may experience struggles with your mental health.

Childhood Causes

The first example of an emotional deficiency that we will examine is more of an umbrella term for various emotional deficits. This umbrella term is Childhood Causes.

If you think back on your childhood, think about how your relationships began in your early life. Maybe you were taught that when you behaved, you received food as a reward. Perhaps when you were feeling down, you were given food to cheer you up. Maybe you turned to food when you were experiencing adverse events that happened during your childhood. Another cause could be the relationship you had with your parents in your formative years. Maybe you grew up in an emotionally abusive home, and food was the only comfort you had. These reasons are entirely valid, and this was the only way you knew how to deal with problems when you were a child. The positive thing is that now that you are an adult, you can take control of your life and make lasting changes for the better.

This example illustrates how mental struggles can lead to disordered eating, and they can also lead to more serious struggles such as depression or anxiety.

These experiences could cause someone to suffer from emotional disorders in adulthood, as it becomes something learned from an early age. This type of emotional deficiency is quite challenging to break as it has likely been a habit for many, many years, but it is possible.

When we are children, we learn habits and make associations without knowing it that we often carry into our later lives. While this is no fault of yours, recognizing it as a potential issue is important to make changes.

Covering Up Emotions

Another emotional deficiency that can manifest itself in adulthood is the effort to cover up our emotions.

Sometimes we would rather distract ourselves and cover up our feelings than to feel them or to face them head-on. In this case, our brain may try to distract us from feeling our true feelings.

When we have a quiet minute where these feelings or thoughts pop into our minds, we can cover them up by deciding to prepare food and eat and convince ourselves that we are "too busy" to acknowledge our feelings because we have to deal with our hunger. Further, we may distract ourselves by playing video games or surrounding ourselves with people. The fact that hunger often arises in this scenario makes it very difficult to ignore and very easy to deem as a necessary distraction. After all, we do need to eat to survive.

This distraction can be a problem, though if we do not need nourishment we are telling ourselves that this is why we cannot deal with our demons or our emotions. If you think you may be avoiding dealing with or thinking about or thinking about or thinking about or if you tend to be very uncomfortable with feelings of unrest, you may be experiencing this type of emotional eating.

CHAPTER 4
Cbt And Unhelpful Thinking Styles

To understand CBT effectively, we must understand the different types of unhelpful thinking styles that exist in people with the disorders that it treats to understand how it can treat them.

What Are Unhelpful Thinking Styles?
Below are the twelve types of cognitive distortions that you need to learn:
1. All or nothing thinking
This kind of thinking is otherwise known as 'black and white thinking.' You tend to see things in either black or white or success or failure. If your performance is not perfect, you will see it as a failure.
2. Overgeneralization
You see one single negative situation as a pattern that never ends. You draw conclusions of future situations based on one single event.
3. Mental filter
You choose one single undesirable detail, and you exclusively dwell on it. Your perception of reality becomes negative based on it. You only notice your failures, but you don't look at your successes.
4. Disqualifying the positive
You discount your positive experiences or success by saying, "that doesn't count." By discounting all your positive experiences, you can maintain a negative perspective even if you find it contradictory to your daily life.
5. Jumping to conclusions
You make a negative assumption even when you don't have supporting evidence. There are two types of jumping to conclusions:
(1) Mind reading: You imagine that you already know what other people are thinking negatively of you, and therefore you don't bother to ask.
(2) Fortune-telling: You predict that things will end up badly, and you convince yourself that your prediction is a fact.
6. Magnification/Minimization
You blow things out of proportion or inappropriately shrink something to make it seem unimportant. For example, you beef up somebody else's achievement (magnification) and shrug off your own (minimization).
7. Catastrophizing
You associate terrible and extreme consequences to the outcome of situations and events. For example, if someone rejects you for a date, it means that you are alone forever, and making an error at work means your boss will fire you.
8. Emotional reasoning
You assume that your negative emotions reflect the reality. For example, "I feel it so, therefore, it is true."
9. "Should" statements

You motivate yourself using terms like "should" and "shouldn't" as if you associate a reward or punishment before you do anything. Since you associate a reward or a punishment with "I should" or "I shouldn't," when other people don't follow it, you feel anger or frustration.

10. Labeling and mislabeling

This kind of thought is an example of overgeneralization to the extreme. Instead of describing your mistake, you automatically associate a negative label to yourself, "I'm a loser." You also do this to others; if someone else's behavior is undesirable, you attach "they are a loser" to them as well.

11. Personalization

You take responsibility for something that wasn't your fault. You see yourself as the cause of an external situation.

12. All at once, bias

This type of thinking is when you think risks and threats are right at your front door, and the amount of it is increasing as well. When this occurs, you tend to:

a) Think that negative situations are evolving quicker than you can come up with solutions
b) Think that situations are moving so quickly that you feel overwhelmed
c) Think that there is no time between now and the impending threat
d) Numerous risks and threats seem to all appear at the same time

How Does CBT Address Unhelpful Thinking Styles?

Now that you understand unhelpful thinking styles, including what they are and how they present themselves, we are now going to look at how CBT addresses and improves upon these unhelpful thinking styles.

The benefit of learning what these unhealthy thinking styles are is that an individual would be better able to recognize when those unhealthy thoughts are happening and then use CBT to control them. When a person has a good understanding of these unhelpful thinking styles, they will be able to interrupt it when it is happening and say to themselves, for instance, "I'm catastrophizing again." When a person develops the ability to interrupt their cognitive distortions, they will then change their thought process into more helpful land positive instead. In the next subchapter, we will learn how a person can challenge their unhelpful thinking styles.

By determining whether your negative thoughts are justified or not, a person can control it and manage their depression or anxiety.

Challenging Your Cognitive Distortions

A person can begin to reshape their negative thoughts into something more factual and realistic once they learn how to identify their unhealthy thinking styles. In this section, you will find all the different cognitive distortions categorized. There are specific questions that I have provided for you to ask yourself to start developing different thoughts.

I want to make a note here for you to keep in mind; changing your thoughts is a process that requires a lot of effort, dedication, and awareness. Don't get frustrated if you are not finding success right away as you have probably had these unhealthy thoughts for a long time. It will take some time to make changes, so don't expect this to happen overnight. The more a person simply just pays attention to their thought processes, the easier it becomes.

Probability Overestimation

If you find that you have thoughts about a possible negative outcome, but you are noticing that you often overestimate the probability, try asking yourself the questions below to reevaluate your thoughts.

· Based on my experience, what is the probability that this thought will come true realistically?
· What are the other possible results from this situation? Is the outcome that I am thinking of now the only possible one? Does my feared outcome have the highest possible out of the other outcomes?
· Have I ever experienced this type of situation before? If so, what happened? What have I learned from these past experiences that would be helpful to me now?
· If a friend or loved one is having these thoughts, what would I say to them?

Catastrophizing

· If the prediction that I am afraid of really did come true, how bad would it be?
· If I am feeling embarrassed, how long will this last? How long will other people remember/talk about it? What are all the different things they could be saying? Is it 100% that they will talk about only bad things?
· I am feeling uncomfortable right now, but is this a horrible or unbearable outcome?
· What are the other alternatives for how this situation could turn out?
· If a friend or loved one was having these thoughts, what would I say to them?

Mind Reading

· Is it possible that I know what other people's thoughts are? What are the other things they could be thinking about?
· Do I have any evidence to support my assumptions?
· In the scenario that my assumption is true, what is so bad about it?

Personalization

· What other elements might be playing a role in the situation? Could it be the other person's stress, deadlines, or mood?
· Does somebody always have to be at blame?
· A conversation is never just one person's responsibility.

- Were any of these circumstances out of my control?

Should Statements
- Would I be holding the same standards to a loved one or a friend?
- Are there any exceptions?
- Will someone else do this differently?

All or Nothing Thinking
- Is there a middle ground or a grey area that I am not considering?
- Would I judge a friend or loved one in the same way?
- Was the entire situation 100% negative? Was there any part of the situation that I handled well?
- Is having/showing some anxiety such a horrible thing?

Selective Attention/Memory
- What are the positive elements of the situation? Am I ignoring those?
- Would a different person see this situation differently?
- What strengths do I have? Am I ignoring those?

Negative Core Beliefs
- Do I have any evidence that supports my negative beliefs?
- Is this thought true in every situation?
- Would a loved one or friend agree with my self-belief?

Using this knowledge, the moment you catch yourself exhibiting these unhelpful thinking patterns, begin to ask yourself these questions to start changing your thought process. Keep in mind that the basis of CBT is the theory that a person's thoughts directly influence their emotions and behavior. By simply paying attention to your thoughts and changing them before it spirals, a person should be able to control both their emotions and behavior.

How to Prevent Procrastination

Since procrastination happens mostly due to a person's unhelpful thinking styles, CBT is a great technique to challenge this because it revolves around monitoring one's thoughts. The first step to using CBT to manage your procrastination is simply trying to be more aware of what you're thinking. Due to our fast-paced society built up of thousands of decisions a day, many people go through their daily lives on auto-pilot to minimize the number of decisions they have to make. They do this to preserve their energy as making that many conscious decisions every day is exhausting. If this is your first time practicing CBT, all I am asking you to do is try to be mindful of your thoughts. Find moments of peace and quiet, and just pay attention to what's going on in your mind. Are you letting yourself be in the present moment, or do you think about the hundreds of things you need to get done this week?

Once you have practiced this a little bit, we will begin learning about unhelpful thinking patterns and styles. People who procrastinate often have adopted numerous unhelpful thinking styles, making them feel like certain tasks are extremely daunting. Combining your newly found mindfulness with unhelpful thinking styles, you will soon be able to identify when you are exercising those unhelpful thinking styles.

CHAPTER 5
Examples Of Cbt

In this chapter, we will be discussing a few tips and tricks to help you start making the small changes you need to incorporate CBT in your lifestyle.

Examples of CBT in Action

In this subchapter, we will be focusing on a real-life example of a person using CBT to treat depression using a case study of an adolescent suffering from depression in Puerto Rico. The purpose of this example is to give you an idea and visualization of what actual CBT sessions look like and what types of benefits you can gain from them. Although depression highly varies in every person, and so do treatment methods, this example can give you a general idea of what a formalized CBT structure would look like.

This case study explores the traits associated with using CBT as a treatment and focuses on showcasing the challenges and high variability in CBT and depression. This adolescent has been diagnosed with MDD (major depression disorder) and will be going through 12 standard CBT sessions. This client is 15 years old and showcasing symptoms of highly dysfunctional attitudes, low self-esteem, and high suicidal ideation. The CBT structure used will be the 12 standard sessions of therapy with an additional family intervention. Scientists conducted this trial based on the statistics that people found about 80% effectiveness when using CBT and/or IPT to treat their depressive disorders. They are looking to prove further how CBT can provide significant changes in a person's depressive symptoms. Let's dive into some details of this case study.

The patient of this case study is an adolescent female 15-years-old of age. She is living with her parents and one younger sibling. The parents of this patient have had some significant marital problems and have been discussing divorce and have separated numerous times. Her mother has a history of mental disorders, including depression and anxiety, while her father has been struggling with bipolar disorder (BPD) and is still going through treatment. There is a history of her father being hospitalized numerous different times due to his serious psychiatric symptoms.

The patient has been suffering in external ways, including failing a few classes in school. Her family was attempting to find a new school for her due to her poor academic performance and social struggles. The symptoms that she has been suffering from are; difficulty concentrating, hopelessness, insomnia, irritability, anxiety, low self-esteem, guilt, overeating, crying, and frequent sadness. She also reported that she has difficulties with relationships due to her negative outlook regarding her academics and physical appearance. She also feels a lot of guilt due to her parent's relationship problems. This patient had a medical history of asthma, obesity, and vision problems. Three years ago, she was diagnosed with MDD and treated on and off for about two years using a blended approach using antidepressants and psychotherapy. Her first depressive episode was triggered when her crush at school rejected her. Her latest episode is heavily related to her academic and social abilities at school and her parents' divorce.

In this case study, the patient who needs treatment uses a manual-based CBT, which has proven to have success in adolescents who suffer from depression. The patient became connected to a clinical psychologist for this study whose job is to direct the CBT sessions and report CBT's effects in this adolescent.

During the first four sessions of the patient's CBT, the therapist focused on teaching her about the relationship and influence of a person's thoughts on their mood and behavior. The therapist taught her about strategies that can challenge your unhealthy thought patterns/cognitive distortions to change them into more positive thoughts. The therapist asked the patient to record their mood at the beginning of every session. The therapist used the log of their moods for discussion. The patient also participated in CBT homework assignments, including logging her positive and negative thoughts and identifying her cognitive distortions. During these first four sessions, the patient's mood had high fluctuation. She cried many times during these sessions and expressed feelings of low self-esteem, sadness, and guilt. The main dysfunctional thoughts that she had were mostly about her traits. For instance, she thought of herself as "ugly and stupid" and that "people look at me because I'm fat." She had anxiety about going to a new school and struggling with whether or not she would be able to fit in. She also struggled with guilt regarding her parents' marriage and thought about her fault that her parents are fighting. By the fourth session, the patient began to succeed at challenging her negative thoughts and replacing them with more positive ones such as "I am capable of making new friends" and "I have a good sense of humor and am very artistic." However, many of her negative thoughts were still persistent, and they focused mostly on her parents' relationship. By the end of four sessions, her self-esteem seemed to be improving as she was beginning to share her artistic abilities with her therapist.

The next four sessions were focused around helping the patient increase the amount of time on activities that she found pleasant; her goal setting and time management seemed to improve her overall mood. The homework that she had to do during these sessions included completing a weekly schedule, logging her pleasant activities daily, creating very specific goals, and making a plan to achieve them—the patient's mood significantly improved by the 5th session. The therapist theorizes that it was most likely due to her grades increasing, making new friends, and having an overall better experience at her new school. She was also getting along better with her new teachers. The patient reported that her depression symptoms were decreasing. The positive experiences that she gained at her new school benefitted her during her CBT sessions. The therapist used those positive experiences as a tool to challenge any unhelpful or negative thoughts that the patient had by providing evidence that proved her theories wrong. For instance, she now has evidence that she can cope in a new school and that she was likable. Therefore, she was able to use this evidence to challenge self-deprecating thoughts that she used to have like "People look at me because I'm fat" or "I am ugly and stupid." She also reported that the number of negative thoughts she's been having had decreased significantly, and she found it valuable that her therapist was verbally reinforcing this.

Through these sessions, the patient found out that one of the main challenges for her when it comes to enjoying leisurely activities or social gatherings was her negative thoughts. These negative thoughts included things such as, "Others will reject me" or "I'll make a fool of myself" and worrying about whether or not her parents will give her permission to do her specified pleasant activities. By keeping track of her scheduled pleasant/leisurely activities, the patient began to manage her time better to include chores and homework. Using this documentation, the therapist and patient evaluated together to have a good balance of chores and responsibilities with pleasant activities. She now knows that doing pleasant activities significantly boosted her mood, so she has to make adjustments accordingly. The therapist also participated in role-plays to convince and negotiate permission with her parents when she wanted to participate in social gatherings or leisure activities. Throughout these second set of sessions, the patient's self-esteem improved continuously as she could vocalize these improvements. She began to have more confidence in her appearance and exhibited healthier behaviors like better posture, grooming, and a general increase in confidence. The patient also reported that she was handling stressful situations much better. For instance, when kids at school were teasing her, she now could simply ignore it rather than beginning to have negative thoughts about herself due to what other people were putting into her head. This example shows us that the patient is beginning to grasp the skills learned in CBT, such as techniques to stop negative thoughts to decrease negative emotions.

The last set of sessions with the client (sessions 9 – 12) focused on exploring how her interpersonal relationships affect her mood. The therapist let her know that they will be focusing on increasing her social support, maintaining it, and improving her assertiveness regarding communication. The patient acknowledged that she has a good social network of supportive people but vented about how one of her friends would often put her down, which led to her negative thoughts about her attractiveness and overall abilities. The therapist helped the patient by examining what expectations she had regarding friendships. The patient showed a more passive communication style, which hurt feelings when she did not continuously meet her emotional needs. Therefore, the first two sessions of this last set focused on helping the patient develop her assertiveness level through role-play exercises. Later on, the patient reported that some upsetting incidents had happened at school. Still, she appeared to be handling those situations better by using the strategies she has studied and learned during the first set of sessions.

Throughout the last few sessions, the patient reported that she was still feeling emotions of sadness, guilt, and anger regarding her parents' divorce. She specifically reported that she was uncomfortable by witnessing her parents' communication problems and how they often spoke badly about each other behind each other's backs. She felt that in an attempt for her parents to communicate with one another, she acted as a messenger. She also talked to the therapist about experiencing emotional and physical abuse between her parents through her experience of living through multiple separations over the last decade. The therapist suggested that they could explore the possibility of having a CBT session with her par, to better communicate with the parents how their communication problems are negatively affecting the patient. The patient agreed to this. During the session, the parents and therapist discussed how the parents' behavior harms the patient's depression symptoms and suggested how they should go through marital counseling or therapy. At the end of the session, the parents admitted that they have significant problems and agreed to go to couples therapy in hopes of working things out.

At this point, the patient has completed the standard CBT session at 12 sessions total. However, the patient was still showcasing depression symptoms at a severe level and still met the criteria for MDD. Therefore the therapist decided to give her additional sessions until she no longer met the criteria for MDD. These four additional sessions focused mostly on the patient's feelings around her parents' separation and divorce. The therapist made sure to teach the patient how to manage her feelings about her parents' divorce to lower its impact on her daily functioning and mood.

Throughout the additional sessions, the therapist found out that the main negative thoughts that the patient has were related to being fearful of how her father may leave their family and never speak to her again. She stated that she was scared of her father remarrying into another family with people she might not get along with. These thoughts were challenged in therapy sessions using CBT, where the therapist asked the patient to find evidence of her thoughts becoming a reality. Through this, the client discovered many of her friends who had similar family situations still had healthy relationships with their parents and new relatives, and she remembered the fact that her father had told her that even if he and his wife had separated, that he would still always be there for her. She then realized that things might be more positive if her parents had just separated, and the number of fights decreased. The therapist also continued practicing role-playing with the patient regarding her father's possibility of leaving the marriage and how it would affect her relationship with her father.

Upon the end of her additional sessions, the depressive symptoms were not in the moderate range and not in the severe range. She also no longer met the criteria for MDD, and her self-esteem had significantly improved, and the therapist reported that her suicidal ideation and dysfunctional attitudes had significantly decreased. During the following months, six months later, and one year later, the therapist noted that she maintained her improvements and that her depressive symptoms were not mild compared to severe.

The therapist focused on closure with the patient to reinforce the patient's improvements in her coping skills and mood during the last session. The therapist also taught her relapse prevention strategies as relapse is a part of the recovery process with many mental disorders. The relapse prevention strategies that the therapist taught her included using CBT strategies to manage her mood, recognizing when she needs treatment, and monitoring her depressive symptoms. The therapist also spent time teaching her mother how to monitor her daughter's depressive symptoms properly and emphasized the importance of helping her daughter seek treatment if symptoms worsen over time.

At the end of this case, the researchers found that the use of CBT had appeared to successfully reduce the patient's depressive symptoms, including her suicidal ideation and dysfunctional attitudes. They found that the number of CBT sessions required to achieve results was 16, four more additional sessions from the standard 12 session structure. Additionally, the patient showed improvements continuously over several months, post-treatment regarding her depressive symptoms, low self-esteem, and dysfunctional attitudes.

The most significant stressor that highly affected the patient's symptoms were the marital problems between her parents. While the use of antidepressants and CBT individually seemed to have been effective in this case study, the use of both may have proven to be a more effective alternative option in terms of achieving recovery and preventing relapse. Moreover, booster sessions post-therapy help improve her even further after the end of therapy. Other additional aspects that may have helped would be family therapy between her parents solely and with her included as well.

This case did a great job illustrating some of the challenges that CBT may face when treating depression with many variabilities. Cases like this one who focused on a patient with significant family issues often require additional stressors and some modifications in the CBT manual to address those significant issues, specifically to offer a complete treatment.

Throughout this case, we found evidence that one of the most effective methods for this patient was interrupting her unhelpful thinking styles and finding evidence to prove that her thoughts are incorrect and that she needed to foster a more positive mindset. It seemed that finding evidence herself created the buy-in necessary to continue using her therapist's skills. The client also participated in homework and worksheets related to CBT, which helped her practice skills outside of sessions, which likely contributed to the treatment's overall effectiveness. I hope this case study did a good job explaining how CBT would work in reality and how the client's effort makes a difference in the treatment outcome. Unlike other talking therapies, CBT requires the patient to practice and do homework outside of the sessions to train and apply the skills she has learned in real life. It seemed like CBT alone was sufficient enough to treat her severe depression, but perhaps with the use of antidepressants or other lifestyle changes at the same time would have sped up and increased the effectiveness of her treatment.

Example CBT Sessions

In this stage of the book, you now understand what CBT, anxiety, worry, and unhelpful thinking styles are. We will move on to some real-life examples of CBT being used to treat anxiety and/or depression. These examples are from real therapy sessions where CBT is being used to help the client reshape their thoughts and change their thinking styles. In these examples, the therapist identifies the client's issues and then teaches the client how to use CBT to change their thoughts.

Example #1 (Session One):

Maria is 40 years old and has two children; Vish and Christina, 17 and 13. She has a husband named Jey, he is a lawyer, and Maria works as a designer at an interior design firm. She is in therapy due to her recurring panic attacks and has a history of depression. Here is the transcript below between Maria and her therapist, Putri.

Maria: I haven't been able to function normally due to my recent panic attacks. My heart begins to race, and I feel like I start to suffocate. I just start to focus on; I'm not sure what...

Putri: Try to focus in on it; give me a feeling of what is happening.

Maria: Well, actually, the panic occupies my entire body. I can't think about anything else. My heart beats fast, and my blood feels hot and

racing as well. I feel like I'm dying. I've already gone to the ER three times because I thought I was in danger.
Putri: So you feel total preoccupation?
Maria: Jey, my husband, was late, and he had also misplaced the car keys. The whole situation was insanity. After I got everyone together, I began to sob. I was crying so much it was uncontrollable.
Putri: And what happened after that?
Maria: Well, after I got myself together, I started getting ready for work. Once I got into my car, I just froze. My heart began racing again, and I felt tingly all over my arms. I thought I was going to faint. My first reaction was to get myself to the ER, so I phoned Jey, but he was still too upset and angry from the incident that morning. He said that I should call someone else to take me to the ER. So I called my only other option, my son Vish, and he left school to take me to the ER. I felt so embarrassed. Once I got assessed by the doctor, she said that there was nothing wrong with me.
Putri: What are your thoughts on that?
Maria: I was confident that there was something wrong with me. The physical feelings that I felt were so real; you know the tingling and heart-racing feelings? The doctor suggested that a psychiatrist would be able to help me.
Putri: So did you go and make an appointment with the psychiatrist?
Maria: Yes, I went through a series of tests, and all of my results came up as negative. I had another appointment with a different psychiatrist the following day, and he prescribed me some medication that seems to be helping a little bit.
Putri: Do you know what kind of medication your doctor prescribed?
Maria: I think they were antidepressants. I'm not completely sure.
Putri: Have you ever been depressed before?
Maria: Yes, think so. I feel like I have battled with bouts of depression throughout my whole life.
Putri: Give me some examples of your battles with depression.
Maria: Well, for example, I feel like I'm battling it presently. My husband is a lawyer, which means that he is pretty much busy all day every day. Vish is a teenager and is also always busy. Christina is becoming an adolescent and at the stage where she feels like her mother is always wrong. I feel like I'm walking on eggshells all the time. I constantly feel like I am worthless. I feel like all hope is lost.
Putri: So you feel like everything is bleak and that there's no hope?
Maria: Yes, it feels like my life is miserable. Almost like a tragedy.
Putri: So it's not just right now?
Maria: No.
Putri: Tell me more about what you are feeling.

Maria: Well, when I was 13, the same age as Christina, that was when my mom passed away from cancer. It felt like my whole life came to an end. I loved my mother so deeply, and I constantly think about what things would be like for my daughter if I --
Putri: If what happened to your mother happened to you?
Maria: Yes.
Putri: What would it be --?
Maria: I wonder about what it would be like for my daughter.
Putri: And you were the same age?
Maria: Yes, I was 13 when my mother passed. Same as Christina's age now. I always think back to all the things I had to do during that time. I was the oldest sibling, so I took care of my dad, sister, and brother.
Putri: What was it like? What did you have to do?
Maria: My father became depressed and turned to drink; I had to care for him. I would be the first to get up out of everyone to get breakfast ready for them. I had to make sure that my father went to work, which meant that I had to wake him up. After that, I would have to make everybody's lunch and then get myself ready for school. I would have to check on my siblings throughout the day as well.
Putri: How do you feel about this?
Maria: Not dealing with our feelings was a constant theme in my family. We just pushed our feelings down and away.
Putri: Pushed them down? I see. What was going on with your dad? You mentioned he was depressed and drinking a lot.
Maria: Yeah. He missed my mom a lot, and I understood, I missed her too. I was the eldest kid, so he took out a lot of things on me.
Putri: How did he take things out on you?
Maria: He would constantly joke about how I was too dumb to go to college. I wanted to go to college.
Putri: So he would criticize you?
Maria: Yes, he constantly belittled me, and I would tell him that he was belittling me. He would get upset then say that he was only kidding.
Putri: How did you feel about this?
Maria: It made me feel awful because you can't get that angry over a 'joke.' I was confused. I took all those feelings and stuffed them as far down as possible.
Putri: Is stuffing down feelings something that you still do now?
Maria: Yes, Jey has that tendency to criticize as well.
Putri: And when you face that kind of criticism, how does it make you feel?
Maria: I get really angry, and afterward, someone usually tells me that it was only a joke.
Putri: What do you do when you get those feelings of anger?
Maria: I stuff the feelings down. I don't like to deal with those feelings.

Putri: If you are stuffing your feelings down the way you do with Jey and your father, how is it impacting you? What price are you paying to stuff your feelings down?
Maria: I don't know.
Putri: I'm not sure either. This could be a possible topic that we can discuss in our future sessions.
Maria: Yes.
Putri: Alright, let's see if I'm on the same page as everything you've told me so far. Please let me know if I'm wrong. You are dealing with many waves of panic, and you've experienced it through the attacks you've been having. These attacks even led you to the ER a few times. It seems like you are going through a few different things.
Maria: Yes, correct.
Putri: Let's start by discussing what we can do about these panic attacks. Then, let's talk about your business of stuffing down feelings and its impact on you.
Putri: I would like you to start noticing when you begin having panic attacks and the exact moment you begin to push down your feelings. We will discuss that in our next session.
In this example, the therapist Putri was able to identify two important issues. The first was Maria's panic attacks; we will continue to explore this in more detail and design a treatment plan since this is impacting her life largely. Once Maria has the skills to keep her panic attacks under control, we can address the next issue: the impact of her depression and anxiety.

Example #2 (Session Two):
Putri: Let's get a better feel regarding your panic attacks. Tell me about the worst incident you've had.
Maria: It was a crazy morning; everybody had just left. Jey left for work, and the kids went to school. Once everyone left, I just started uncontrollably crying. Somehow, my crying ended, and I began getting ready for work.
Putri: Let's try something here. Could I ask you to please close your eyes and sit back on your chair?
Maria: Yes, sure.
Putri: (During this time, Putri explores Maria's thought process and feelings related to the incident. She used an imaging technique to guide her into noticing the thoughts she normally wouldn't pay attention to. This exercise aims to help Maria see that her thoughts and emotions are connected and how it influences her physical behavior, like her panic attacks.)
Maria: I got into my car as I was about to leave for work. Suddenly, I felt lightheaded. I got scared because I thought the panic attack was happening again. My heart began to beat very quickly, and I started to

breathe heavily and very fast. I thought I had to go to the ER because I had a heart attack. I was scared that I wouldn't make it to work. I thought that I had to get help. I felt like my lungs were closing in on me.

Putri: (Putri identifies that Maria is having a catastrophic appraisal of the situation by her describing that she thinks she is dying again and is having a heart attack. Putri wants to make Maria understand that she is not a passive victim during her panic attacks. If she were able to look at her situation from a new perspective, she would have the ability to cope differently. She can change her outcome)

Putri: In this situation, everybody had left for school or work, and you felt a sense of relief. Then you had those feelings of panic?

(For Putri to help Maria see the connection between triggering stimulus, thoughts, emotions, and behavior, Putri decides to use the metaphor of a visual clock to help Maria see her situation. Noon is the situation, 3:00 are her apprehensive feelings, anxiety, and fear, 6:00 is the catastrophizing thoughts that happen automatically, and 9:00 is the behaviors of a panic attack.)

Putri: So the thoughts you were having: "Is this happening again? I'm losing control!" Then, being unable to get to work and looking for help, "Who can I call to help me?" It sounds like it is a cycle.

Maria: Yes, a vicious cycle.

Putri: That is something we can look into. (With Maria's agreement, Putri helped her explore ways that Maria can begin to monitor her thoughts)

Putri: One action that you will need to start doing is to note down when you begin to have anxiety feelings. Be very specific when this happens. Then, we will be able to keep a record of the specific anxiety-inducing situations.

Maria: Yes.

Putri: (The focus of treatment here will be to bring Maria's panic attacks under control. Putri will do this by teaching Maria how anticipatory fear plays a role like panic attacks. Putri will also help Maria with the following; managing her symptoms, paying attention to warning signs, interrupting her inner critic, breathing exercises, relaxation training, cognitive restructuring (to help control catastrophic thinking styles), interpreting anxiety symptoms accurately, and learning coping techniques.

At the end of session two, Putri has decided that she will implement the following cognitive behavioral therapy treatment plan for Maria:
- Learning about the role that anticipatory fear plays in panic attacks
- The nature of panic disorders
- Skills to help manage anxiety/panic symptoms
- Cognitive restructuring (changing unhelpful thinking styles)
- Graduated exposure to panic stimulus
- Coping technique practices

Example #3 (Session Three):
Maria: So, last Tuesday when I went into Christina's room in the evening to let her know dinner was ready, she started screaming at me about --
Putri: (Continues to monitor Maria's anxiety by focusing her attention on Maria's thoughts and feelings during the situation)
Putri: Help me get a better understanding of what happened with Christina. How did you feel after you walked into her room?
Maria: Well, I felt like the blow-up wasn't my fault. I felt that it was unfair. I felt I couldn't have done anything about it. I began to think that in this family, nothing I do is right.
Putri: What happened next?
Maria: I left her room. I was able to see how I'm starting to get riled up about it. I felt that my chest was starting to close in on these feelings.
Putri: (Putri notices that Maria tends to interpret her feelings of irritation and anger, as tenseness and anxiety. She describes them in physical terms such as a tight feeling in her chest.)
Maria: My whole body felt very tense, but I tried to calm myself down.
Putri: Did you feel the sensation of your heart racing again?
Maria: Yes, my heart was racing, and I felt suffocated.
Putri: What happened this time?
Maria: I just left the situation by leaving Christina's room.
Putri: (After doing a quick review of the remainder of Maria's thoughts, feelings, emotions, and behaviors, Putri decided to focus on Maria's hyperventilation issue. She wants to help Maria regulate her bodily changes during hyperventilation and give Maria a sense of control. Putri decides to use a method called diaphragmatic breathing as a coping tool for Maria.)
Putri: When humans experience panic attacks, one thing that tends to happen is that they begin to breathe very quickly. That is the act of hyperventilation. When people experience this type of breathing pattern, it tends to make their body tenser. Many of the feelings you are having during your panic attacks; tingling, dizziness, hot and cold flashes, are all symptoms related to how you are breathing. Therefore, if you learn to control your breathing, this could help you stop the vicious cycle of hyperventilation. Let's take a minute to practice breathing exercises.
Maria: Sure.
Putri: Great. This exercise will give you an idea of what you can control. Please sit back in your chair in a comfortable position. Then, close your eyes.
Putri: Start by taking a slow and deep breath, filling your chest, and hold it. Slowly breathe out and pretend that you are trying to cool down a spoonful of soup by breathing on it but not spilling it. Feel the warmth and calmness of the soup. Think about the things we talked about

regarding how being tense contributes heavily to the vicious cycle of hyperventilation.

Putri: (In the next step, Putri decides to focus on Maria's panic disorder's cognitive component. Putri decides to examine Maria's thoughts using an anecdote.)

Putri: Another part of this vicious cycle that we've been talking about are the kind of thoughts that you are having. For us to both get a better understanding of them, let's go back to the situation with Christina and examine what you thought and how you felt at each stage.

Maria: Alright.

Putri: Let's pick up at the moment where you had gone into Christina's room. What did she say?

Maria: She began yelling at me about always invading her privacy. I thought this was so unfair. I didn't do anything wrong by telling her dinner was ready.

Putri: So, she was attacking you at random?

Maria: Yes, I didn't do anything. After I left her room, I thought to myself how I can never do the right things for my family and how I am always wrong. I can never be right, and I'm worthless.

Putri: So these thoughts of "I never do anything right, and I am never appreciated" are those a part of your vicious cycle?

Maria: Yes, exactly.

Putri: I'd like to look into two components of this. The first is, what are the things you can do to alter your thoughts? The second is, where are these thoughts and feelings coming from? Let's begin with trying to break out of that cycle, and then we will move onto figuring out where your feelings are coming from.

Maria: Okay.

Putri: Walk me through what those thoughts were.

Maria: So, I thought her yelling at me wasn't fair. It's not like I did anything wrong. All I did was to let her know dinner was ready. When I began to leave her room, I started thinking that this is the way it always is. I am always in the wrong, and I don't do anything right. I'm a complete failure.

Putri: (When Maria describes these thoughts, Putri identifies them as automatic thoughts. She will help Maria find the evidence that supports or doesn't support her thoughts to help Maria see things from a different perspective)

Putri: Is it true that you are a complete failure?

Maria: No, absolutely not.

Putri: Exactly, you are not a complete failure.

Maria: No, I am not.

Putri: In what ways are you not a complete failure? (Putri is challenging Maria to find evidence to prove that she is not always failing.)

Maria: I've done so much in the past, and I had to raise my siblings when I was still a child. My dad kept telling me that I wouldn't be able to go to school because I was too dumb. I made sure that I went to school anyway and paid for it entirely myself.
Putri: So you paid your way through school?
Maria: Yes.
Putri: So when your mom died, you had to take care of your dad and your siblings.
Maria: Yes.
Putri: Then you went to school?
Maria: Yes. My dad was extremely depressed, and all he did was drink. He kept telling me that I was too dumb to study interior design. To prove him wrong, I got into an art school and studied it.
Putri: So you were still able to do it despite the things he said about you?
Maria: Yes.
Putri: Do you have any other examples of why you are not a failure?
Maria: Well, Vish got into a good college and is about to go, so that's awesome. The kids are pretty good.
Putri: How about your work? Do you feel like you are failing there as well?
Maria: Not at all; I've been working there for over two years already.
Putri: So, based on your assumption that you are a complete failure, does that fit the description of someone who accomplished all those things?
Maria: No, I guess not.
Putri: (The discussion of supporting evidence which is consistent with the fact that Maria is not a failure, has given her hope. She began to cry softly at this realization)
Putri: Do the assumption of you being worthless and a complete failure match with the evidence of who Maria is?
Maria: No.
Putri: (To validate Maria's reactions, Putri decides to help Maria appreciate how the feelings she had are not only normal but appropriate given her childhood and the history with her dad)
Putri: The tears that I see you have right now are a sign of how much you are in touch with your feelings.
Maria: Yeah, they are.
In the next three sessions with Maria and Putri, they used various CBT techniques to help Maria develop control over her panic attacks. They used diaphragmatic breathing to manage her hyperventilation and anticipatory fear. They identified Maria's cognitive distortions and her tendency to catastrophize and practice fact-checking her thoughts to determine what is true and what is just a thought. Putri encouraged Maria to practice those coping skills every day as a form of an experiment to see what worked with her and what didn't.

To analyze the last three examples, we were able to see how the therapist identified areas where Putri was displaying unhelpful thinking styles. In this case, she was catastrophizing. We were able to see how the therapist uses CBT to identify these thoughts, some of which are automatic, and help the client find their evidence inconsistent with those thoughts. The breathing techniques help soothe anxiety symptoms and help you refocus your attention from the anxious thoughts to simply managing your physical symptoms. You may have noticed in the above examples that the client and therapist must be working as a team. There needs to be full cooperation and dedication to practicing new skills, thought processes, and coping techniques. CBT is only effective if the client is practicing it throughout their daily life.

CHAPTER 6
Preventing Relapses With Cbt

Many people that are on their journey of recovery worry about losing the progress that they've made by having an anxiety relapse. A previously suffering person but has their symptoms reduced wants to make sure that they keep these positive changes as long term as possible. This desire is very understandable, as slipping back into old habits will cause a loss of improvement. Luckily, there are many methods and ways to prevent relapses and control lapses.

The first thing we should learn about is the difference between a lapse and a relapse. We define a lapse as a brief return to old and unhealthy habits. It is very common and normal and often happens from fatigue, low mood, or stress. We define relapse as a complete return to old ways of thinking and behaving during anxiety bouts. Individuals who have a relapse tend to be doing all the same things they used to be doing before learning new managing anxiety methods. Keep in mind that although lapses can lead to relapses, they don't necessarily have to. You have the power to stop a lapse from turning into a relapse.

Here are some examples showcasing a lapse compared to a relapse:

Let's say that you had a phobia of riding in a car. If you have been going through CBT, you have probably learned that it is not the best idea to avoid riding in a car. Instead, you have been taught to practice breathing exercises, practice coping thoughts, and gradually work your way up to riding in a car.

So if one day you were out with a group of coworkers and one of them offered to drive the group to dinner, and you avoided the situation by making an excuse and walked home instead, this would be called a lapse.

If you entirely went back to your old and unhealthy routines such as being late to work due to you avoiding to ride in a car or missing social events because they are too far to walk to, this would be called a relapse.

So when does a lapse turn into a relapse? Usually, the things you say to yourself after having a lapse can lead you to get back on track or lead you into a relapse. If you perceive your lapse as a sign of failure, you may likely give up and have a relapse. However, if you perceive your lapse as a slip-up or a mistake that you could recover from, then you likely will not have a relapse.

If we went back to our car, phobia example:

If you ended up avoiding riding in a car with your coworkers by making an excuse and walked home, but at the end of the day, you said: "I fell into my old habits again, I better start practicing some CBT techniques this week to get myself back on track."

This event would result in your lapse ending, and you continue to face your fears and healthily manage your anxieties.

However, if you ended up avoiding the car situation with your coworker and at the end of your day, you said, "All the hard work I put into managing my anxiety around cars was a complete waste! I am now right back where I started because I'm such an idiot. I guess there is no cure, after all, might as well stop trying."

This situation would result in your lapse turning into a relapse. It will likely cause you to stop practicing CBT any further, and you will return to your old and unhealthy habits.

Although relapses are common when it comes to recovering from anxiety, there are a few causes that could play a role in a relapse:

- Stressful life events that happen to you during or after recovery can cause a relapse. These events can include things like relationship changes, family conflict, and grief.
- Stopping early in treatment is another way for a relapse to happen. Since anxiety isn't a quick fix, you need to stick with your treatment plan for months after you start feeling better to reduce the risk of relapse. Failure to do this may cause you to slip back into old habits.
- A feeling of inability to cope using your prescribed anxiety management strategies is a common cause of relapse. If you feel like the strategies you were taught and given aren't working, seek help from your therapist or counselor to figure out a new strategy to get on track. Most people have to experiment with different strategies to find one that works best for them.
- Changes in your lifestyle or physical health also play a huge role in relapses. If you have physical illnesses like heart disease or diabetes, it could increase your risk of worsening anxiety. Big lifestyle changes can also create lots of stress, which prevents you from taking the time to practice managing your anxiety.

How to Prevent Relapses

The best way to recover from a relapse is to prevent one in the first place. By taking all prevention measures and being prepared, you are at a much lower risk of relapse than someone unprepared. Keep in mind that it is normal to have lapses and relapses, but your mindset dictates whether you get back on track or stay in a state of relapse. Below are a few tips on preventing lapses and relapses:

- **Practice, practice, and practice!** The best way to prevent a relapse is to frequently practice your CBT knowledge and skills or whatever treatment plan you learned. If you are always practicing, you will be in a good position to handle whatever life throws in your ways. You can fit in practice by making a schedule for yourself, consisting of which skills you will practice every week. This practice may include breathing exercises or

challenging unhelpful thinking styles. Get friends or family to hold you accountable for practice.
- **Know your red flags!** People are less likely to have a lapse or relapse when they know when they are most vulnerable in having one. For instance, most lapses and relapses happen during times of stress or big change.
-
    - Make a list of warning signs that indicate when your anxiety is increasing. This list can include:
        - Increased feelings of anxiety
        - Increased responsibilities at work, home, or school
        - Increased anxious thoughts
        - Arguments with family/friends
        - Major life changes (e.g., death, childbirth, wedding, moving)
        - Avoidance of activities (e.g., social events, exercise, going outside)
    - Make a plan on what to do when you encounter your danger signs in terms of coping. This plan includes:
        - Practice CBT more frequently.
        - Taking some time-outs for yourself to practice things like breathing exercises or mindfulness
        - Relaxing (hanging out with friends, reading a book, watching a movie)
- **Coming up with new challenges!** Just like everyone around you, you are a work in progress. There are always different ways and strategies that you could use to improve yourself to make life more fulfilling and enjoyable. A good technique to prevent relapses is to challenge yourself to work harder on further anxiety. You can start by making a list of situations that are anxiety-inducing and begin to work on them. People are less likely to fall back into old habits if they continue to challenge themselves by learning new and different ways to manage their anxiety.
- **Learn from your lapses!** Keep in mind that it is normal to have lapses occasionally. At times of greater stress, people are more vulnerable to a lapse if they are still learning to cope with anxiety. The good thing about this is that you can learn a lot about yourself from these lapses. You can use your lapses as an opportunity to figure out what the situation was that led to a lapse. Knowing that situations make coping more difficult for you can help you prepare for the next time. You can create a plan to help you cope with more difficult future situations.

- Was it due to you having anxious and upsetting thoughts?
- Was your anxiety very high at the time?
- Were you doing something different?
- Did you know that the situation would be difficult, or was it a surprise to you?
- **Knowing the facts!** In this chapter, you have learned that what you are thinking after a lapse largely affects your chances of a full relapse. If you think you are a failure, you are more likely to give up and fall into a relapse. Consider these things:
    - It is not possible to entirely fall back into 'square one.' You cannot unlearn all the techniques or skills taught to you through treatment (e.g., CBT). Being at square one means experiencing anxiety but having no knowledge of how to deal with it. Since you have started your treatment and have learned many skills during it, you know how to handle anxiety, and therefore, you are not back to 'square one.'
    - People who relapse can 100% get back on track. Even if it had taken you months to practice ways to manage your anxiety symptoms, it wouldn't take you just as long to get back to where you were before the relapse. Once you get back to practicing your anxiety management skills, you'll be on your way to mastering it again in no time.
- **Be kind to yourself.** Keep in mind that lapses and relapses are normal and part of the process. Don't punish yourself harshly during moments of weakness as it doesn't help you in any way. Instead, it is more useful to understand that people make mistakes sometimes. If you don't speak to someone else like that, you should not be speaking to yourself like that. It may be very helpful to have a lapse to understand your weaknesses and learn where to focus your practice.
- **Reward yourself!** Ensure you are taking the time to reward yourself for the hard work to manage your anxiety. To encourage motivation, give yourself a treat now and then. Rewards can range from buying yourself something nice, going out for a nice meal, or just taking some time to pamper and relax. Learning to manage anxiety is hard work, so make sure you are celebrating all your progress.
- **Exercise:** Researchers have found that regularly exercising can be just as effective as medication when treating depression and anxiety. Exercises cause an increase in the 'feel-good' brain chemicals in the brain, such as serotonin and endorphins. These chemicals also trigger the growth of new brain cells and connections similar to what antidepressants do. The best part

about exercise is that you don't need to do it intensely to benefit. Even a simple 30-minute walk can make a huge difference in a person's brain activity. For the best results, people should aim to do 30 – 60 minutes of aerobic activity every day or on most days.

Social Support: Like I mentioned earlier, having a strong social network reduces isolation, which is a huge risk factor in depression and anxiety. Make an effort to keep in regular contact with family and friends (ideally daily) and consider joining a support group or class. You can also opt to do some volunteering to get the social support you need while helping others.

- **Nutrition:** The ability to eat healthily is imperative for everyone's mental and physical health. By eating small meals that are well-balanced throughout the day, you can minimize your mood swings and keep energy levels up. Although you may crave sugary foods due to the quick boost of energy that it can bring, complex carbohydrates are much more nutritious. Instead, complex carbohydrates can provide you with an energy boost without a crash at the end.
- **Sleep:** A person's sleep cycle has strong effects on mood. When a person does not get enough sleep, their symptoms of depression or anxiety may get worse. Sleep deprivation causes other negative symptoms like sadness, fatigue, moodiness, and irritability. Not many people can function well with less than seven hours of sleep per night. A healthy adult should be aiming for 7 – 9 hours of sleep every night.
- **Stress reduction:** When a person is suffering from a lot of stress, it intensifies their depression or anxiety and increases their risk of developing more serious depression or anxiety disorders. Try to make changes in your life that can help you reduce or manage stress. Identify which aspects of your life creates the most stress, such as unhealthy relationships or work overload, and find ways to minimize their impact and the stress it brings.
- **Practicing Gratitude:** An important method of overcoming depression and/or anxiety is to practice gratitude frequently. When you are in a moment of stress, anxiety, or depression, take some time to think about all the things in your life that you appreciate. The things you can think about include all the worldly things that you have like your home, your computer that you use all the time, or even just your favorite type of coffee that you have at home. Practicing gratitude also includes expressing gratitude towards your positive qualities. For instance, being grateful for your strength, your intelligence, and any other good qualities that you know you have. This method is very simple and gives people

a better perspective on their lives. People are often stuck in the moment of distress and can't take a step back to see the bigger picture. Removing yourself from the distress in a moment and thinking about all the things you are grateful for makes a huge difference in changing your mindset. Remember to be kind to yourself, even in the darkest moment.

Recognize the Mind-Body Connection: You may be wondering how these two seemingly unrelated things (the inner world and the outer body) can be considered related. In this section, we will look at how the mind and body connect and cannot be disconnected. To illustrate this, we will look at an example that involves food and eating.

Over time, your body learns that eating certain foods (like those containing processed sugars or salts such as fast food and quick pastries) makes the body feel rewarded, lively, and happy for some time after you eat these foods. When you feel sad or worried, your body senses this and looks for ways to remedy these negative feelings. Your brain then connects the mind's emotions with the reward that it knows that it can get from eating certain foods. As a result, it decides that eating these foods will turn their inner state from negative to positive and make it feel better. As a result of this process that happens in the background without you being aware of it, you consciously feel a craving for those foods (like sugary snacks or salty fast-food meals), and you may not even be aware of why you are craving them. This process all happens in a brief second in the subconscious mind. If you decide to give in to this craving and eat something like a microwave pizza snack, your body will feel rewarded and happy for a brief period. This act reinforces the concept believed by your brain that craving food to make itself feel better emotionally has worked.

If you feel down and guilty that you ate something that was unhealthy, your brain will again try and remedy these negative emotions by craving food. This example shows how a cycle of emotional eating can begin without being any the wiser.

Because scientists and psychiatrists have come to understand this process in the brain and the body, they know that the mind and body are inextricably connected. Food craving and even being overweight can often indicate emotional deficiencies or emotional struggles. For this reason, it is essential to address the underlying issues when trying to deal with depression or anxiety. By dealing with the root causes of the problem, you can prevent it from recurring. If you try to break free of anxiety for some time without looking deep within to find the causes of the struggles you are having, the chances of falling back into your old state are very high. Therefore, it is necessary to address the root causes to end your struggles once and for all.

This is another great way that we can come to understand issues like depression and anxiety, as they manifest themselves in the physical body. If you find yourself experiencing food cravings, take a look deep within and find out the underlying issues.

Like I mentioned earlier, the best way to get back on track from a relapse is to simply not have one. However, relapses and lapses are normal throughout a person's recovery journey, so if you find yourself having a lapse or a relapse, get some help. This strategy could be in talking to a therapist, a friend, or a family member. The quicker you seek help, the easier it will be to come back from that relapse. Remember, every little bit of progress is still progress, and that is not all entirely lost due to a relapse. You still have a plethora of knowledge and skills that you've gained throughout treatment, and you can once again put those skills to use.

Although Cognitive Behavioral Therapy is the most effective type of speaking therapy out there, it is important to try other treatment plans to further your recovery. More important than trying out different types of treatment is refusing to give up. Many treatments aren't quick-fix solutions; they require you to do exercises, practice, and apply them in real life. Continuing to exercise skills and techniques you have learned to overcome anxiety and depression is the main pillar. Even if you have recovered from your mental disorders and have gone months, even years, without incident - it is still important to set aside some time to practice the techniques that worked for you. This time is important to prevent lapses that could lead to a full relapse. By continuing to practice skills that have worked for you, you will be well-equipped to deal with a potential lapse if something traumatic or sudden change happens to your life. Preparation is key.

CONCLUSION

For all the knowledge you have learned for this book to work, you must be consistent with practicing CBT. Most people don't see the effects of CBT visibly until 4 – 5 weeks in, sticking with it and not giving up is something you need to pay attention to. Always start slow and get the fundamentals down. Start by simply just paying more attention to your thoughts, and you will slowly be able to see the patterns of your negative thinking. The moment you can realize this, you can begin to interrupt your negative thinking. The hardest part of the whole CBT process is to change your mind from being on autopilot to paying attention to thoughts. That act of doing that is tiring, so some people do not find success with CBT when they don't practice. However, the mind and brain are a very malleable function in the body; the brain can adapt to whatever is healthiest and best for your body. By practicing and actively paying attention to your thoughts, your habits will begin to change, and you'll slowly start to see the error of your thinking styles.

I want you to pat yourself on the back for taking the initiative to learn more about how to treat mental disorders. This learning is not an easy task. When a person is suffering from the symptoms of common conditions like anxiety or depression, it's hard for them to think clearly and strategically. The fact that you found the motivation to purchase and read this book and finish it and a considerable achievement. You learned in-depth about cognitive behavioral therapy and how it treats anxiety and depression. This information about CBT is one of the most important takeaways as CBT can provide people with the right tools to combat their negative thoughts.

So what's next beyond this book? Well, if you think you have a mental disorder, please ask for help. This help doesn't have to be in the form of a therapist, but just talking to friends and family can offer you the guidance you need to take your next step. If you are thinking of getting a therapist, reach out to multiple, and get a consultation. Make sure that the therapist you choose has experience treating specific things that you are feeling. Do also make sure that you and this therapist get along, and you are comfortable with how they are approaching your treatment. Keep in mind that most therapies require you to practice outside of the sessions. Be prepared to take the extra time so you can practice everything you learned from therapy.

I hope this book helped you learn everything you need to know regarding cognitive behavioral therapy and mental disorders. As someone who has experienced this for many years, I have one thing to say to you. Don't be so hard on yourself, and it will get better for you. Taking the first step in finding help will start a chain effect in overcoming your mental disorders.

Everything will become easier once you equip yourself with the right tools to handle any situation that life throws at you. Don't give up.

DESCRIPTION

Have you ever wondered how you can find solace and peace from anxiety and depression? Have you ever wondered how you can break free from negativity and follow your dreams? Have you ever wondered if there is more out there for you? Are you feeling stuck and are struggling to get out of your slump? Are you someone that feels like their mental disorders always burden them? Have you been looking for a solution and a way out? This book will provide you with this and so much more!

CBT has shown significant results for up to 75% of people who use it as treatment. The effectiveness level rises to 90% if combined with other methods.

This book will teach you how to apply CBT to your mental health care, and it will also teach you other methods that help treat mental disorders. By combining CBT with other treatments like meditation and lifestyle improvements, the entire treatment set's effectiveness rises significantly. Upon opening this book, you can expect to find the following information;

- What cognitive behavioral therapy is
- The history behind Cognitive Behavioral Therapy
- The modern-day uses of CBT
- How CBT works
- Different types of CBT techniques
- Benefits and drawbacks of CBT
- How to start small with CBT
- Anxiety disorders, causes, and symptoms
- Depression disorders, causes, and symptoms
- The science behind depressive disorders
- Different types of depression
- The benefits and drawbacks of choosing CBT as treatment
- How to use CBT to manage your anxiety and/or depression
- Other methods that also help to manage anxiety and/or depression
- How to prevent relapses
- Effects of untreated depression, anxiety, and other mental disorders
- Where to turn for assistance after reading this book
- Real-World Examples of CBT sessions

This book will explore the theories and functions of Cognitive Behavioral Therapy and how it works to treat disorders like Anxiety and Depression. We will start this book by learning more about how CBT works when used and how it compares to other therapy types. We will then learn about what anxiety is, its symptoms, and different types. With all of this information and more, you will be well-equipped to begin taking control of your life.

When a person is suffering from psychological distress, the way they perceive certain situations can become contorted, this could cause negative behaviors. By learning about CBT and how it can help you, you can begin to change these thoughts and start seeing things.

The mind and the brain are very malleable and are always ready and willing to change. The brain can adapt to whatever is healthiest and best for your body. By practicing and actively paying attention to your thoughts, your habits will begin to change, and you'll slowly start to see the error of your thinking styles.

Overall, this book aims to teach you how to use CBT; its purpose is to educate you on all topics related, so you understand why CBT uses the strategy that it does. Understanding that, people are more likely to stay committed to the process than give up if they don't see results right away.

www.ingramcontent.com/pod-product-compliance
Lightning Source LLC
Chambersburg PA
CBHW071452070526
44578CB00001B/317